SHAPES FOR WOODTURNERS

SHAPES FOR WOODTURNERS

DAVID WELDON

B.T. Batsford Ltd · London

First published 1992
© David Weldon 1992

Typeset by Tek-Art Ltd, West Wickham, Kent
and printed in Great Britain
by The Bath Press, Bath
for the publishers
B.T. Batsford Ltd
4 Fitzhardinge Street
London W1H 0AH

A catalogue record of this book is available from the British library

ISBN 0 7134 7031 3

CONTENTS

INTRODUCTION

Woodturning, like most crafts, comprises four main elements: equipment, materials, technique, and design.

When you start, you learn about the first three of these, but then you are usually left to your own devices as to what to do next. This is as unreasonable in turning as it is in any other craft, and can result in a loss of interest as well as a certain uniformity in output from a wide range of turners, as attendance at many local craft fairs will confirm.

Few escape this creative dead end.

In this volume are 500 designs for 'stand alone' turnery, i.e. where each piece is complete in its own right, rather than part of some larger project. I have also offered some ideas about developing your own variations on these basic themes. You should never again need to make the same piece twice. In addition, if you are selling your output, you will be able to produce 'limited editions' for many years without diminishing your pool of designs to any significant extent.

Whether you are a novice or a professional, there is something here for you; something that will give you ideas suitable to your needs, and set you challenges appropriate to your abilities.

PART I

THE TECHNIQUES

SAFETY

Safety procedures are not just desirable, they are essential, and take precedence over everything else. Woodturning is very safe as long as you follow a few very simple rules:

1 Always have a suitable fire extinguisher on site.

2 Make sure that the power supply OFF switch is where you can get at it if anything goes wrong with the lathe. It is no good having it on the wall behind the equipment, it must be to one side with the power line firmly fixed to the wall.

3 Ensure that the lighting to your work area is good. A double fluorescent in a safety cover is the best, and this should be situated over your head rather than directly over the lathe.

4 Make sure that you know how to maintain all your tools and equipment, and, just as important, make sure you actually do it.

5 Never adjust anything while the lathe is running.

6 Keep the area under your feet clear of debris. A dust extractor is a most desirable feature of any workshop, on both health and safety grounds, but I have yet to find an effective method of attaching one to a lathe. If you have one, you will find it quick and easy to keep the whole of your work area clean.

7 Do not store your tools in a rack on the wall behind your lathe, as I have seen in some illustrations. The idea of someone leaning over their work for a fresh tool terrifies me.

8 Always wear some form of eye protection. There are two types, goggles and a visor. I recommend a visor as this gives the extra benefit of protecting the whole face from an irritating barrage of wood shavings, and is the first line of protection for both nose and mouth. Even if, like me, you wear spectacles, you must still wear eye protection.

9 When working with abrasives, or with timbers likely to produce irritant dust, wear a dust filter that covers the nose and mouth.

10 Shoes must have non-slip soles, and uppers tough enough to protect your feet against a dropped chisel. High ankles that go up inside the trouser leg are a blessing, as they stop your footwear filling up with shavings.

11 Clothing must be tight fitting around the cuffs and lower arms, and should have nothing that could conceivably catch in any part of the lathe. By far the best thing to wear is a one piece overall with a front that zips right up to the neck.

12 If your hair is long, wear a hat. It is certain that at some stage you will lean over your work while it is in motion, and I leave you to work out what happens when hair gets caught in a lathe. It is not a bad idea to wear a hat anyway, just to keep yourself clean.

13 Use only the correct tool for the job, make sure it is sharp, and do not force it into the work.

14 After switching off the lathe, wait for it to stop, do not slow it down with your hand.

15 Use only the kind of heaters that do not have exposed elements or flames. This is not only because of the fire hazard, but also because of the possibility of a dust explosion.

16 No smoking.

EQUIPMENT

BACKGROUND

The biggest mistake you can make when buying a lathe is to buy cheap on the basis that if you like turning you can upgrade at a later date. This policy will ensure that you give up turning within months, or even weeks. Machines are cheap for good reason: they are noisy, smelly, too light, badly made with poor bearings, and vibrate a lot. They are unpleasant to use and produce poor results, which make it almost inevitable that the buyer gives up turning.

There are many good lathes on the market, with dozens of attachments for each of them, and a wide range of different turning tools and other bits and pieces. A comprehensive guide to this minefield is *John Sainsbury's Guide To Woodturning Tools And Equipment* (published by David and Charles in the UK and Stirling in the USA).

Rather than duplicate this detailed catalogue, I intend to provide guide-lines to help you find your way through this maze. The point I would make at the outset is that the person with the most equipment does not necessarily do the best work. Certainly there are times when only one specific attachment will do the job, but the expert is the one who really knows the basics. If you have a good solid lathe, a few simple attachments and tools, and learn how to use them properly, you will be a better turner, and have more enjoyment, than the person with a room full of equipment, none of which is properly used.

You will also understand how everything works, and be in a position to make your own jigs for doing jobs as you want them done, rather than buying something that does the job the way somebody else wanted it done. In short, you will become a thinking turner, better able to scale the heights of possibility that would otherwise remain a mystery to you. You have only to look at the work of some of the great turners to see what can be done when you know your job.

THE LATHE

There are essentially two types of turning: spindle work and bowl work. The former requires a lathe with a long bed, but not necessarily any great diameter; the latter needs a big diameter, but no great length. If you are just starting, you will probably have some preference for one or the other, but you should get a lathe that does both.

Short bed lathes will allow you to make bowls and plates up to around 500mm (20in) diameter, but will only allow about 400mm (16in) between centres. If you are only doing bowls, this kind is hard to beat, but I regard it as a lathe for the specialist. In the early stages it is better to get something that will make a smaller bowl, but allow longer spindle moulding. You should be looking for at least 800mm (32in) between centres and a bowl turning facility of 300mm (12in) diameter.

The way the bowl turning facility is set up varies from make to make. In some machines you may have to start moving parts around if you switch from one function to the other. You should check your intended machine to ensure that it is easy to change functions, and that, after changing it round, everything is solidly locked. My own has a separate outboard bed for bowl turning, which makes it consistently rigid as everything is permanently bolted in place. This does have the disadvantage of needing separate face plates for each side.

Once you have decided on the type of lathe you want, you have to decide the make. (Everyone has their favourites and those they dislike intensely, and it would be extremely unwise for me to attempt to pass on my own prejudices.) You must take certain sensible precautions, and the first of these is to go to a store specializing in turnery. It is no good going to your local tool shop and ordering the one they happen to have the catalogue for. You must be given a choice of makes and see the one you want to buy. There is no substitute for getting your hands on the beast and feeling for yourself the quality, or lack of it! I would offer the following guide-lines for judging a lathe:

1 It must be solidly built. Imagine you have got a 200mm (8in) square, 900mm (36in) long lump of oak in it. Does the lathe look as if it will stay in one piece while you cut the oak down, or is the machine the more likely of the two to be reduced in size at the end of the operation?

2 All the moving parts must move smoothly in the direction they are supposed to go, and not move at all in other directions. Having moved, they must lock tight in their new position.

3 It must have good adjusting handles that are easy to get at, especially when there is a large piece of work in place. You should not need to go looking for Allen keys or spanners every time you want to do something.

4 There should be a range of speeds. Commonly, the range is from about 500rpm to 2000rpm, but if you are to do a lot of bowl work, speeds down to 250rpm or less are desirable. The speed change should be easily accessible and simple to use.

5 If the machine is floor standing, the stand must be built to the same heavy quality as the lathe, or if it is to be bench mounted, you must get a good heavy bench to go with it. It does not matter how good the lathe is if you then screw it to the top of an old table.

6 Make sure that you know exactly what comes with the lathe, and that spare parts and accessories are easily available. Check this with other suppliers of turning equipment.

7 How does it compare with the other machines in the shop? Are you getting it because it is the only one you can afford, or because it is the one that is best for your needs? If you cannot afford the one you want, consider waiting a while until you can.

8 The tool rest must be nice and heavy: it will have to take a lot of punishment. Most turners have a shape of tool rest they swear by, but each swears by a different shape! I suspect it is simply a matter of what you learn on. If there is an option for one longer than about 300mm (12in), make sure it is supported in two places.

9 Listen to it running. Bear in mind that you may be spending hours at a time standing at the machine, and if it sounds like an electric drill on overtime, neither you nor the lathe will last long.

10 If you are buying your equipment second hand, and are not experienced with machinery, take someone with you who is, even if you have to hire them. The small cost can be thought of as insurance.

DRIVES AND CHUCKS

FOUR PRONG DRIVE Often only the two prong version is supplied, but this can split the wood, and does not hold the work as well as the four prong version. It is important to keep the drive flanges sharp.

FACE PLATES My own are 125mm (5in) and 50mm (2in) diameter, and I have a range of home made, wooden step-up and step-down plates for other sizes, but the standard 75mm (3in) or 100mm (4in) are both perfectly satisfactory. If the lathe has a separate outboard for bowl turning, you will need different face plates for this.

SCREW CHUCK This is like a small face plate with a screw through the centre, and is needed for pieces where you need to be able to work the end as well as the sides. Ensure that the screw is parallel-sided, rather than tapered at the end like a normal wood screw.

COMBINATION CHUCK The idea behind a combination chuck is that it can be adjusted to hold virtually any piece of work. It is a face plate, screw chuck, pin chuck, expanding and contracting collet, cup chuck, collar chuck, etc., all in one. Highly desirable, but extremely expensive. There are at least a dozen on sale, all of which perform a similar range of functions. If you can afford one, get one.

LIVE CENTRE FOR TAIL STOCK Dead centres are usually provided, and for my money are quite useless. My own live centre is heavy duty with a removable centre point. The advantage of this is that I can make my own wooden inserts to support special jobs. You can also buy a cup or ring centre for any work that is liable to split if supported at a single point.

DRILL CHUCK It normally fits in the tail stock, but as long as the morse taper in both stocks is the same, it can be used in the head stock to hold very small work.

BASIC TOOLS

Turning tools can be made from a number of different materials, but if you consider the expense, time and effort you are putting into setting up in turning, the idea of saving a few pounds on chisels is absurd. I must unhesitatingly recommend high speed steel. These tools stay sharper longer, and are less prone to damage by overheating.

ROUGHING OUT GOUGE – 35-40mm (1½in) A deep fluted gouge, with the end cut square across, and the bevel ground at 45 degrees. It is used to remove the bulk of the waste from a piece of timber, and is the first tool you should learn to use. You can get quite close to the finished shape with this gouge.

SPINDLE GOUGES – 19mm (¾in) and 10mm (⅜in) They are shallow fluted and should be the shape of a fingernail across the end, with the bevel at 30-35 degrees.

SKEW CHISELS – 25mm (1in) and 12mm (½in) They are ground at an angle of 70 degrees across the end, with the bevel at 40 degrees. They can cut anything except a concave surface and must be considered to be the workhorse of the woodturning craft.

PARTING TOOL – 5mm (¼in) diamond It is used primarily for removing the work from the waste when the turning is done, but most turners find that there are other uses, such as very small bead work. There are three types. The best for parting is the fluted, but it can only be used for parting. The flat-sided is cheap, but has poor clearance. The diamond is wider in the middle than at the top and bottom, has good clearance, and is the most versatile of the three.

BOWL GOUGE – 20mm (¾in) This is a completely different tool from the spindle gouge. It must be long, heavily built, with the flute narrow and deep, the end rounded, and the bevel cut at about 50 degrees. It is used for all the rough work on both the inside and outside of bowls.

ROUND-NOSED SCRAPER – 20mm (¾in) This is used for inside work where the curve is fairly abrupt. The angle of the bevel is almost vertical, about 80 degrees.

SEMI ROUND OR DOMED SCRAPER – 25mm (1in) Rather like the round-nosed scraper, but the end curve is much less severe. The bevel is once again at 80 degrees. It is used for the inside of large objects, where the curve is gradual.

SQUARE-END SCRAPER – 25mm (1in) Used for face plate turning where a large flat area is to be cut, such as a plate. The bevel is at 80 degrees.

Most face plate and spindle work can be done with the tools listed above. There is, however, a range of other tools needed for special projects. By the time you get round to wanting them you will undoubtedly be sufficiently experienced to choose the tools you need.

MEASURING EQUIPMENT

Very little measuring equipment is needed. I would limit it to internal and external calipers, a large and small one of each, and a vernier caliper with a depth gauge. The only other piece of equipment for which there is much call is a wall thickness gauge, but ordinary external calipers are sufficient for most purposes.

TIMBER

HOW TO BUY

Timber is your raw material, and the responsibility for learning about it is yours, and yours alone. The following few paragraphs only touch the surface of what there is to know. I shall show you where to start, but then you have to get out and handle the timber yourself, and get some sort of feel for it. This is not difficult, but it will take time. In your early days, buy sparingly, and as you learn more, buy in larger amounts.

Finding good timber at a fair price is not as easy as it should be. There are a lot of mail order firms who, between them, supply a good range of timber. For people who need very little, or those who are not very mobile, these firms provide an efficient way of buying timber. My problem is that I like to see the lump of wood I am buying, and I would strongly recommend that you do the same. Not only does it mean that you are taking complete responsibility for your purchasing, but visiting woodyards and sawmills is fun.

By far the best approach is to find a sawmill, and keep in touch on a regular basis. This way the staff at the yard get to know you and your needs, and I think it safe to say that regular customers usually get the best service. If you have the facilities to convert large pieces of timber, I would recommend that you buy whole logs or planks wherever possible. If you buy bowl turning blanks, you are paying the yard to select and prepare the timber, and they will cut it to their convenience, not yours. If you buy a log, you can do with it as you wish, taking your time to consider how to put it to the best use. You might, for example, want to use the sapwood that the woodyard may well have removed when preparing the blank. Similarly, a piece of timber that the yard might have used for a large bowl, you might decide to turn into fifty egg cups (or vice versa). None of this changes the fact that if you want to make half a dozen bowls, each from a different timber, then bowl turning blanks may be the best way to do it.

What you actually look for in a piece of timber is another matter altogether. The first thing to know is how to look. If you are buying timber in the plank, take a block plane with you, so that if the timber has been standing a long time, and is discoloured on the outside, you can run the plane across it to look inside at the grain, texture and colour. Be especially careful about splits that will limit the size of piece you can make, even when you are buying blanks. The fact that someone is selling a piece of timber as a potential bowl in no way guarantees that there is not a split up the middle of it.

Be reasonable about your requirements. It is no good complaining to the yard owner that all the boxwood logs have a twist in them, or that all the ebony logs have a split down the middle. This is just the way these timbers are.

Finally, check the moisture content. The yard will be able to tell you how the timber was dried, and advise you on how long it will be before you can use it, depending on your storage facilities and the particular use to which you are going to put it. You can safely expect help from a reputable sawmill, but try to go mid-week, not in the middle of a busy Saturday morning.

There are other sources of timber, one of which is observation. If you see anyone taking a tree down in their garden, try to get the trunk from them. This is important for the rarer timbers like laburnum and lilac, or the fruitwoods. I have a local tree surgeon who sometimes comes up with the odd bits of timber, which cost me the occasional glass of beer.

There are many books about timber on the market, produced mainly for the furniture trade. They cover such subjects as the structure of timber, how to dry your own, how to store it, and so on. It is not necessary that you read, learn and digest all this material, but you should try to acquaint yourself with the subject if you can.

THE TIMBERS

The comments that follow are simply intended as general observations about three dozen or so of the hundreds of timbers available. The timber you buy depends entirely upon the piece of wood in front of you. If it is suitable for your purposes, buy it, if not, do not.

APPLE A clean, even-textured timber, mid-brown in colour, often with a pink or red tinge. It turns easily, and is well suited to tall elegant shapes such as long-stemmed wine goblets.

ASH Pale cream, with a very open texture. Not widely used in decorative turnery, though it can be used green for bowls. It has the extremely tough, rather elastic properties that make it ideal for the handles of tools. Very rarely planks with a ripple pattern become available, and these can be very attractive.

BEECH A hard, close-grained timber with a slight pink colour. It turns very easily, and is widely used for mass-produced household items, but its uninteresting texture and colour make it of little use in decorative items.

BLACKWOOD African blackwood is dense and dark, but not always black as the name might suggest. It turns well, but is extremely expensive. Australian blackwood is hard and dark red-brown, but tends to be used less often for turning.

BOX True box is creamy yellow in colour when new, but darkens with age to the most glorious yellow-brown. It is only available in fairly small logs, and the grain can sometimes be very difficult, but it takes detail like no other timber. It is superb for combined turning and carving. Avoid boxwood substitutes – they are no substitute as they have neither the grain nor the colour of real boxwood. They also tend to be much softer.

BURRS Many timbers, such as oak, walnut, elm and yew, regularly produce burr timber. A burr occurs where the growth of the tree has got out of control, and the result can be thought of as hundreds of tiny knots. The result of turnery with burrs can be quite astonishing, but burrs are just about the most difficult thing to work with that there is. I wasted a lot of burr timber in my early days because I just did not have a good enough technique. Buy burrs whenever and wherever you can, but keep them until you know you are good enough to use them.

CHERRY There are many varieties of cherry. The common cherry is brown, with a hint of orange, and a clean grain that makes it one of the easiest timbers to turn. As a timber for beginners it is hard to beat.

CHESTNUT It looks similar to oak, for which it is often substituted in furniture, but the silver grain of oak is missing. It turns rather well.

COCOBOLO The colour is strong red, and it turns well, but the dust is poisonous, and the oil it secretes can stain the skin for weeks.

EBONY The colour and texture of ebony is very variable, so take care in selecting it. It varies from jet black to dark brown, and splits very easily. Apart from the mess it makes, it is one of my favourite timbers. It was widely used for the highly ornate turnery that was so common in the nineteenth century.

ELM One of the toughest timbers there is, and favoured by the wheelwrights of old, it is light brown with a coarse irregular grain. As it is a very difficult timber to turn well, it is best avoided by beginners, but can produce extremely fine results, especially for bowls. A good timber for green turning.

FRUITWOODS Most of the fruitwoods have their own entries in this list, but as a general rule, they are the best timbers for beginners to start on. They are easy to obtain, reasonably cheap, turn easily, have interesting colour and grain, and take a wide variety of finishes.

GRAND PALISANDER Often sold as Mexican rosewood, it is a wonderful timber to turn and finish, and has a spectacular cream and rose contrast in the grain.

HOLLY This tough, close-grained, white timber is becoming increasingly used for what is almost the woodturner's equivalent of porcelain. Very thin, almost translucent work can be done. One word of warning, however: the timber can have a very unpleasant grey tinge, making it look dirty.

HORNBEAM A tough timber, with indistinct grain and a pale, sometimes slightly dirty looking colour. It turns well, but is not particularly interesting.

IRONWOOD Jet black, virtually no visible grain, cold, heavy and as hard as a lump of pig iron. It turns beautifully, but destroys tools in the process.

KINGWOOD A member of the rosewood family, with very distinctive purple and cream stripes. It turns easily, but choose simple shapes that allow the beauty of the timber to predominate.

LABURNUM A rich green-brown timber, with lots of interesting flecks in it. Because it is easy to turn and produces spectacular results, it is becoming increasingly expensive as turners fight for the little there is.

LAUREL A hard dark timber, very pleasant to work, but only available from a few suppliers. The Australian laurel is often sold as Australian walnut. It has a colour and texture very similar to walnut and you should not let the confusion of names put you off.

LIGNUM VITAE A very hard, heavy, dark and expensive wood, much used in the sixteenth and seventeenth centuries for ornamental work. Many of the old wassail bowls are made from it. It polishes well, but always seems to me to have a slightly gloomy feel to it.

LIME A soft, cream wood with no real figure. It turns very easily and is a superb timber to carve, so for anyone who wants to mix these two skills in a single piece of work, lime is definitely worth serious consideration.

MAHOGANY Like teak and rosewood, mahogany is a name that includes timbers from the nasty and utterly useless to the very beautiful. The colour varies from rich red through to dull brown, depending on quality. Care is needed when working a good piece of timber, but the effort is always well rewarded. If you ever see Honduras mahogany, buy it at once, and sort out what to do with it afterwards.

MAPLE/SYCAMORE These two timbers are so alike that they are completely interchangeable. Almost white in colour, the grain is usually clean, and turns very easily. However, turners tend to be interesterd in those timbers where the grain is *not* clean. The two main ones are Fiddle and Bird's Eye, both of which are very highly sought after and therefore expensive. In Fiddle, sometimes called Flame, there is a quite exquisite ripple through the plank. Bird's Eye maple has lots of little knots, making it look like a brown and cream peacock's tail. Both these timbers are shown to their best advantage on large, flat pieces where the main interest is the timber rather than the shape.

OAK Throughout the world, many different timbers are sold as oak, but the true English oak is *Quercus robur*, while the main American oak is *Quercus alba*. Some 'oaks' sold are not even of the *Quercus* family, so check before you buy. The colour is generally golden brown, with a distinctive silver figure. Its coarse, open texture makes it difficult to turn, and it is avoided by many turners. Brown oak is just ordinary oak that has been stained dark brown by the beef-steak fungus, *Fistulina hepatica*.

OLIVEWOOD A soft timber that turns and finishes easily, commonly used for food bowls. Its grain can be anything from dull, boring brown to an exceptionally beautiful mixture of cream and rich brown.

PADAUK (PADOUK) It turns well, but the grain is uninteresting, and the colour a rather bright orange-red, although it does darken with age.

PEAR Another timber ideal for the beginner, pinky brown in colour. Being clean-grained, it turns very easily.

PINE – see **SOFTWOOD**

PLANE The *Platanus occidentalis* is the American plane, often called American sycamore, and the *Platanus acerifolia* is the London plane. The timber is usually pale and uninteresting, but when properly cut there can be a very beautiful brown figure giving the effect of lace. Turns very nicely, but the lace figure can be overpowering on larger items.

PLUM Yet another timber that is ideal for the beginner. It is brown, often with streaks of red and purple, with a clean grain, so it turns very easily.

PURPLEHEART An unusual timber that is dark cream when first cut, but a few days' exposure to air will turn it purple.

ROSEWOOD This single word covers such a multitude of timbers that they would need a book in their own right to do them justice. They vary from pale pink to deep purple, but the colour of the timber often changes with exposure to air or sunlight. While the results can be brilliant, the colour change can be extremely disappointing. Many of them produce highly irritant dust, and the wearing of dust masks is essential. Turning qualities vary considerably from piece to piece.

SATINWOOD A heavy wood, pinky cream in colour, with a very fine grain, deep within which is a wonderful, subtle figure. This and the timber's natural lustre give it its name.

SOFTWOOD Very variable in colour and texture, depending on its source. It is becoming increasingly used in commercial turnery. I hate it. It is often suggested that beginners use it to practise on because it is easily available and cheap. I cannot agree with this, and recommend the fruitwoods, which are much more interesting and not wildly expensive.

SNAKEWOOD It has a very unusual and interesting grain and the colour is deep red-brown with dark markings. It is one of the world's most expensive timbers, but many turners think that the cost is justified by the results.

SPALTED TIMBER Spalting results from the tree falling, and being left on the ground to become infected by fungi. The resulting coloured stripes produced in the timber are completely unpredictable, and quite extraordinary. Spalted timber can be difficult to turn because the rotting that has begun to occur can make the hardness variable. It is one of the most highly prized of all turnery timbers.

SYCAMORE – see **MAPLE**

TEAK A wide variety of commercial timbers fall under this heading. I do not find it a rewarding timber to work with as it produces a lot of irritant dust. Most turned teak seen in Britain is cheap, mass-produced material imported from south-east Asia.

WALNUT A clean-grained, rich brown timber that is a great favourite because of the finish that is possible. It turns beautifully. Australian walnut is not walnut, but is a member of the laurel family, which is why it is sometimes called Australian laurel. It turns very well. American black walnut has a very distinctive brown colour quite different from English walnut, and it can be found in very large clean pieces, suitable for huge items.

YEW The grain varies from clean to completely wild, and the colour from pale yellow-orange to purple. When the grain is clean, it works very easily, but as the grain gets wilder, turning gets more difficult.

ZEBRANO A quite extraordinary timber, which at its best is black-and-white striped, as its name would suggest. To get the best from this timber, stick to simple shapes that show off the grain to its best advantage.

TECHNIQUES

BEFORE YOU START

In all your work in 'stand alone' turnery, you must remember that the product is going to be handled. People will pick the object up, look inside and underneath, and generally examine all parts of the piece, because handling a turned wooden object is pleasurable. The whole of your design, planning and execution must take this into account. I do not think it unreasonable to ask of a piece of work, 'If it were turned upside down, would there be anything about the quality of workmanship or finish that would make the inversion apparent?' If the answer to the question is 'yes', then there is something wrong. A similar question could be asked, perhaps a little more fancifully, about the object being turned inside out. Treat all parts of each turned object as of equal importance.

Most things can be adequately explained in books, but technique is difficult. An hour with a good turner is worth a shelf full of instruction manuals. What matters is feel. There are a number of books on the market that do an excellent job, considering this limitation. The authors of these books recognize, as do I, that personal tuition may not be possible. The guide-lines below should be considered only as an outline of the basic techniques, enough to get you started safely. Once you have mastered the use of these basic tools, you will be applying the principles that underpin all other aspects of turning.

SHARPENING

When I first took up turning, in nineteen-sixty-something, I went to a general woodwork evening class. The tutor was not a turner, and did not know how to sharpen turning tools, so I had to scrape. When I found out how to sharpen them, I learned how to cut.

The aim when sharpening tools is to get a single bevel (rather than the double bevel on ordinary woodworking chisels). Some turners say that you should have a slightly concave face to all your tools, but I have never found this to be necessary. There are many ways of sharpening tools, and the method that follows has always served me well enough. I begin with a grinder, using a moveable tool rest to get the angle I need for the particular tool. This gives me the general shape that I want for the bevel. Then I use a linisher to polish the face of a scraping tool, or a diamond stone to give a fine cutting edge to gouges and chisels. The advantage with a diamond stone is that it does not need oil, and I have an aversion to getting oil anywhere near my work. Once you have an edge, you keep going back to the stone or linisher every time it starts to go. You should never need to go back to the grinder.

The scrapers must be sharpened so that there is a burr left on the upper edge, as on a cabinet scraper. It is this burr that does the work. First polish the upper face of the scraper until it is absolutely flat right up to the cutting end, then apply the face of the tool either to a stone or a linisher (or belt sander). This produces a burr on the top edge of the tool. The type of burr you make depends on the work you are doing. If you are removing a fair amount of timber, use the coarse burr generated by a grindstone. If you are finishing a piece of work, use the much finer burr of a linisher. You can tell a properly sharpened scraper, because it will not produce sawdust, but rather small, clean wood shavings.

MOUNTING THE TIMBER

There are so many different ways of mounting timber, depending on the particular job in hand, the piece of timber, and the equipment that you have, that I do not intend to go into all of them. Instead I shall cover only the three basic methods, i.e. between centres, the screw chuck and the face plate.

BETWEEN CENTRES In spindle moulding, the timber is supported at both ends, allowing you to work freely along the whole length of the timber. The basic drive fitted into the head stock is the four prong centre. It is important to understand that it cannot simply be hammered into the timber. Drill a small pilot hole in the end of the timber to take the centre point, then make two saw cuts, at right angles to one another, to take the flanges of the drive. In order to avoid the possibility of splitting the timber, it is important that neither of these cuts should follow the grain, but should cross it. The drive centre is then tapped home lightly with a mallet.

At the tail stock end, drill a small hole in the centre of the timber to take the point of the centre. Tightening the tail stock is equally important. Beginners tend to tighten it as much as possible, on the basis that, if you jam the wood in hard enough, it will stay put. As well as damaging the lathe, this creates two problems: first, it can produce severe stress in the timber, splitting it, and second, it will cause the work to flex as it spins, making accurate cutting impossible.

SCREW CHUCK For relatively short work where you need to be able to work not only around the circumference of the work, but also in at one end, the screw chuck is the basic drive. The best kinds of screw chuck have parallel threads rather than the more common tapered thread. To mount the work, make a clean cut across the end of the piece of timber to be used, and pre-drill a hole in the centre, rather smaller than the size of the screw. Then simply screw the chuck into the work until it is tight. The crucial thing about using this chuck is that the end of the timber that goes against it must be perfectly flat. If the piece of timber you are working with is very irregular, as is often the case if you are working with logs, you can still use the tail stock to hold the timber firmly while you rough it down to size.

To avoid the hole in the base you can either work with the timber about 35mm (1½in) too long, or buy one of the many excellent combination chucks, which, although expensive, do make life rather easier.

FACE PLATE The face plate is used wherever the diameter of the work is large, and much of the work is to be done at the end rather than the side. The most obvious example is a bowl. First cut the blank as near round as possible on a band saw, and plane the face that is to be the top absolutely flat. Mount it on a face plate with the intended base of the bowl facing outwards.

Finding the centre of a blank is often a problem, yet the solution is simple. Get a piece of drafting film and, using a compass, draw several concentric circles on it about 20mm (¾in) apart. Whenever you need to find the centre of the blank, simply lay the sheet on it and centre it using the appropriate circle.

Often the timber has to be worked on, then removed from the lathe and remounted the other way round. If the remounting is not correct, clearly the two ends of the object are going to be worked around different centres. Perhaps the best way to start, which requires no extra specialized equipment, is to cut a foot on the base, about 10mm (⅜in) high, before removing it from the lathe. Unscrew the work from the face plate, mount another flat piece of timber on the face plate, and turn a recess that exactly fits the foot you have cut, and is deep enough to take 6mm (¼in) of the foot. Glue the work into the hole and allow it to dry before continuing.

Another simple method is to turn into the base a recess, exactly the same diameter as the face plate and about 6mm (¼in) deep, while the work is still on the lathe. Remount the work with the face plate inside this recess. When you have finished the work, plug any screw holes in the normal manner, or glue baize in the recess. The disadvantage with this method is that it limits the depth of bowl you can turn because the screws can get in the way.

Once again the combination chucks have collets, which expand to fit into a recess, or contract to fit round a foot. Sooner or later you will want one of these, but the options above are low-cost, low-tech.

POSITIONING THE TOOL REST

The most important factor in the use of tools is the placement of the tool rest. You must set it so that it is clear of the timber, yet it must support the tool as close to the back of the bevel as possible. If you have a large gap between the timber and the rest, not only is it dangerous, but your control of the tools is reduced. It is essential that you revolve the timber a couple of times by hand before turning the lathe on to check that you have clearance all round. As you turn the work down, keep stopping it and move the tool rest closer to the work. *Do not* adjust it while the lathe is in motion.

USING THE TOOLS

Before using any tool for the first time on spinning timber, practice on a stationary piece. This way you can safely hold the tool in place with one hand while you take a close look at the cutting end. You will see for yourself, better than in any set of photographs, how the timber and the tool interact. Practice any cutting movements in the same way until you get used to the flow of them.

To begin with you will hold the chisel in something approaching a death grip. This is not necessary. As time goes on you will learn to relax. You will also make mistakes, and get the odd catch or two, but this is to be expected. You cannot possibly hope to take up any skill and get it right first time. Accept errors as part of the learning process, and do not let them affect your confidence.

ROUGHING GOUGE The most important factor in using this and any other gouge is that the bit of the gouge touching the tool rest should be the same part of the cross-section as that doing the cutting. To put it another way, the gouge must be supported directly behind the point at which the cutting is taking place. If you try any other way you will find that the cutting edge digs in and leaves a large hole.

Once the timber is spinning in the lathe, place the gouge on the tool rest, at right angles to the timber, with the handle well below the level of the tool rest. Move the handle of the chisel forward until the bevel meets the timber, then move the handle up until the cutting edge starts to work. The gouge should then be moved along the tool rest, cutting as it goes. As you move the gouge, roll it so that the cutting is shared by the whole of the cutting edge, and is not all done by one little bit in the middle, which will quickly go blunt.

Knowing when you are down to a clean cylindrical shape is simply a matter of paying attention. Do not forget to use your ears: they can tell you more about the state of the moving timber than your eyes.

SPINDLE GOUGE As with the roughing gouge, the most important thing is to ensure that the part of the tool supported on the rest is directly behind the part doing the cutting. Keep the handle lower than the tool rest, and offer the gouge up to the work so that the first part to make contact is the heel of the bevel, then raise the handle so that the cutting edge comes into play. When you are cutting hollows, choose a gouge smaller than the curve, and let it flow around the shape. In spindle moulding, you must always turn from the larger diameter to the smaller, never the

other way. In effect what you must do is cut with the grain rather than against it.

SKEW CHISEL While it is true that some turners produce fine work without being able to use the skew chisel, I think it safe to say that most of the best turners have taken the time to master it. What is certain is that when you can use the skew, it will repay you handsomely. The most important thing is that it should not be treated like a scraper, i.e. it must not be held flat on the tool rest and pushed horizontally into the timber. It is the turner's equivalent of a plane.

The two parts of the chisel that are never used for this planing cut are the corners. The cutting is done with the central portion of the edge, and is always carried out on the upper third of the timber. Set the tool rest slightly above the centre of the work, and offer the chisel up to it, with the handle down. You will find that you have to bring the tool to the timber, not at right angles, but at 20-30 degrees off line, with the pointed corner at the top. With the work stationary, experiment to see how the angle at which you hold the chisel affects which part of the cutting edge does the work, and how the height of the tool rest affects the part of the timber that is cut.

Now turn the lathe on and try it. Do not set the lathe at its slowest speed thinking that this will make life easier, it will not. Practise on a 50-75mm (2-3in) diameter piece of clean timber, at about 1500rpm. Make sure you put a good piece of timber in, not a piece of rubbish. I would suggest something like cherry, which turns very easily and is quite cheap. Once you have mastered going in a straight line, try your hand at curves. Remember that the skew can only do convex curves, not concave.

In cutting convex shapes, such as beads, the corners (or heel and toe) of the skew chisel are used. Mark the extremes of the bead with a pencil, and set the tool rest slightly above centre. The first two cuts are made with the chisel on its edge, with the toe (long corner) at the bottom, and the handle at right angles to the work. Push it into the wood and make a cut, with the toe, about $\frac{1}{8}$in (3mm) deep.

The bead is now cut from its highest point, towards its lowest i.e. the turning is done 'downhill'. Turn the chisel over so that the heel is now at the bottom, and, to cut the right hand side of the bead, rest the chisel on its bottom left hand corner so that the face of the chisel is tipped about 45 degrees from the vertical towards your left, and the handle about 20 degrees below the timber. Move the chisel towards the timber so that the heel comes into contact with the centre of the bead, and make the cut by moving the chisel to the right, at the same time moving it into an upright position. At the end of the cut the handle should still be below the tool rest, but the face of the chisel should be vertical.

The left hand side of the bead is the mirror image of this movement. A good way to understand what is going on is to put a tennis ball in the lathe *with the power off*, and practise moving the chisel over its surface. The only part of the cutting edge to come into contact with the ball, or the timber, is the lower half. Once the cut moves up the cutting edge, there is the danger that it will tip the chisel and the toe will remove a chunk of timber.

PARTING TOOL The parting tool should be held with the handle very slightly lower than the cutting edge, and simply moved at right angles through the timber. A common fault is to let the tool move towards the waste as you cut. This will make the base of the object convex, giving it an interesting rocking motion when you put it down on a flat surface. If you are going to err either way, make the base very slightly hollow as it will then stand solidly.

BOWL GOUGE Used for bringing both the outside and inside of face plate work to shape, the technique for the bowl gouge is so similar to that of the spindle gouge that if you can understand the use of one, you can understand the other.

For outside work, mount the bowl on the face plate with its base outward, and the tool rest set across the corner of the blank, roughly parallel to the final line of the outside of the bowl (for the mathematically minded, set the tool rest parallel to the tangent of the mid-point of the bowl's curve). Check that you have all-round clearance by turning the blank by hand, then start the lathe and remove the corner. As soon as a gap of about 20mm (¾in) appears between the rest and the work, stop the lathe and move the rest closer.

If the timber has been mounted with the grain parallel to the axis of the lathe, cuts should be made from the large diameter to the smaller, as with spindle moulding. If the grain is at right angles to the axis of rotation, then the cut is from the smaller to the larger diameter. It is particularly important that if the shape of the side of the bowl is such that it is fatter in the middle than either the top or the bottom, you still take your cut directions from the diameters, rather than thinking in terms of working from rim to base or vice versa.

To turn the inside of a bowl, remount it as discussed above. Begin by drilling a hole in the centre of the bowl to the depth required. To do this, set the tool rest parallel to the face of the work, and at such a height that the point of the gouge is in the centre of the blank. Hold it horizontally out from the centre and, running the lathe at slow speed, push it into the timber. Stop when the depth of the hole is slightly less than the depth of the finished bowl. Alternatively, use the Jacobs chuck and a 12mm (½in) drill bit.

With the tool rest still set along the face of the blank, cut the rim of the work until it is smooth. Once the rim is established, you can begin to remove the waste from the inside of the bowl. As usual, the gouge should be held handle down, and the cutting done slightly above the centre line of the bowl. Start cutting in the middle of the work with the cut following the line of the final inside shape, not the top of the blank.

The first cut will remove only the corner of the top of the hole, and each subsequent cut will remove a little more. If the timber has been mounted with the grain parallel to the axis of the lathe, cuts should be made from the small diameter to the large. If the grain is at right angles to the axis of rotation, then the cut is from the smaller to the larger diameter. As with cutting the outside of the bowl, you must take your cut directions from the diameters, rather than thinking in terms of working from rim to base or vice versa.

Once it is safe to do so, move the tool rest so that it is parallel to the line of the cut, with its tip actually inside the bowl. Regular bowl turners have a range of specially made curved tool rests so that they can keep the gouge supported as close to the bevel as possible.

SEMI-ROUND SCRAPER The scraper is only used when the bowl has been cut very much to size using the gouge. The major difference between using the scraper and the cutting tools is that the handle of the scraper is held a fraction higher than the cutting edge. This will feel very strange at first, perhaps even dangerous, but it is both correct and perfectly safe. The reason for this is that it is the burr on the top face of the scraper that actually does the cutting, not the corner where the top and face meet.

The scraper must always be held with the whole of its flat face touching the tool rest, it must never be tipped onto a corner. Scraping takes place at the horizontal diameter of the work. It is obviously crucial that the curve of the bowl is less sharp than the curve of the tool. If the curve is too severe for the semi-round, then use the round-nosed scraper instead.

Finally, remember that the scraper is not a blunt instrument used for removing vast quantities of wood, but a fine finishing tool for cleaning the surface of a piece of work that is already the right shape.

The direction of cut should be worked out in exactly the same way as for the use of the bowl gouge.

ROUND-NOSED SCRAPER This is used in exactly the same way as the semi-round scraper, except that it goes into narrower situations, such as small bowls with a very sharp curvature. The main thing you will need to get used to is that the cutting edge is often a long way from the tool rest. Work up to this gradually; do not make life difficult for yourself by making your first project 100mm (4in) deep and 25mm (1in) diameter!

FLAT-NOSED (SQUARE-END) SCRAPER The method of using the flat-nosed scraper is the same as for the other two, but it is used for turning large flat areas such as the bottoms of plates.

NON-STANDARD TECHNIQUES

Traditionally turners make objects which are essentially functional, or at least look functional. The techniques below require that you change the way your mind approaches the work. You have to get away from the idea of function, and start to think more like an artist or sculptor. The purpose becomes to produce an object which has existence as its function.

REASSEMBLING Making a reassembled object, something which works particularly well with bowls, is extremely easy, yet it often has people puzzling about how you achieved the effect. The finished object is symmetrical, so it looks turned, but it is symmetrical about the wrong axis, so it could not have been turned!

Turn up a bowl with a simple shape, such as that on page 48, bottom left. Do not flatten the base, but instead carry the curve on round. The important thing is the shape of the rim. The top of the rim should be about ¼ in (6 mm) thick, and perfectly flat. The edges, where the rim meets both the inside and the outside of the bowl, must be absolutely clean and square. Once the bowl is turned, take it to a band saw with a very sharp, very fine blade, put it rim-side down on the table, and cut it in half.

Now glue it back together, but instead of gluing the two cut edges together, glue the two rim edges together. When the join is fully dried, sand the top flat. Rather than do this by rubbing the new rim with sandpaper, tape some fine abrasive paper to a piece of glass and rub the work on the paper.

MICROWAVING This very recent development in turnery, when it works, produces quite extraordinary work. The first step is to turn a very thin bowl. Keep the space very simple, and the wall thickness down to about ¹⁄₁₆ in (1.5 mm). Once the bowl is turned, put it in a microwave for a few seconds and the timber will quickly heat up and become rather plastic. You will now be able to bend the walls of the bowl into strange shapes. The exact length of time in the oven depends on the particular piece, and the only way to find out is to stop it every ten seconds and try.

You will need to experiment quite a lot before you get the hang of it, so don't use your best timber to start with. The other thing to watch is that the more interesting the grain of the timber, the more difficult it is to get it to stay in one piece. However, if a piece does split, use the split to your advantage, bending part of the bowl one way, and the other part in a completely different plane.

WEDGING I call this wedging just for the sake of something to call it, rather than because wedges are always used. At its simplest a bowl is turned, cut in half down the centre, and the two parts glued to a solid wedge of a contrasting timber. Thus the final piece is a wedge, standing on its thick end, with two halves of a bowl glued either side like saddle bags.

More sophisticated versions of this could have a cylinder stuck through the base, or perhaps a cone. Taking this a stage further, there is no need for the inserted piece to be either regular or functional, or even timber. The impression can be created of a piece of turnery which has been crashed into by some object, or perhaps even two pieces of turnery which have somehow become fused.

UNDERWORKING Most turners seem to be unable to underwork a piece of timber: they feel bound to force the whole thing into the shape that they want. If you have an unusual piece of timber such as a small burr or piece of crotch wood, or even a piece from the top of the root, take your time with it, study it. Quite often you will find that there is a natural shape to the timber, and your function as a turner then becomes more akin to that of a wood carver or sculptor.

With such timber you need to work out the minimum amount of work you need to do to produce a sucessful piece.

FINISHING

WHY USE A FINISH?

In deciding upon a finish for a particular project you need to consider the two main reasons why you need a finish at all. First, it is to protect the timber from the various problems it will meet in the course of its existence, such as heat, water, chipping or handling. You have to select the kind of finish that will provide the most suitable protection for the item you are making. For example, you should not use polyurethane varnish on a drinking vessel, and it would be equally inappropriate to put olive oil on a gatepost finial.

The second purpose of finishing is to maximize the beauty of the timber. To me this means that the finish itself is secondary to the timber, and if someone comments about it before they talk about the wood, then something is wrong. I have a friend who works as a lighting engineer in a theatre, and he takes it as a gross insult if someone comes up and compliments him on the way he lit the set as the audience should not have noticed the lighting. So it is with the best kind of finish: it creates a glow that comes from within the work rather than a surface flare.

Unfortunately a good finish (good in the above terms, that is) has two drawbacks. The first is that it takes time, and if you are producing commercially, this puts the price up. The second is that some people *like* their timber to flash, finding the deep subtle shine simply a bit dull. As with anything else, you have to match the product to the user both in terms of style and cost. The quick finishes have the benefit of being cheap, the complications are that they are less durable, and that the protection and enhancement functions are often in serious conflict.

However desirable one may be, the universal finish does not exist, and a major part of the skill of the woodturner is selecting the right finish for the job in hand. The best turnery in the world can be spoiled by the wrong choice. You would be well advised to go out and buy as many different finishes as you can, and just try them out for yourself. Keep all these experiments to assist you in the future when it comes to making decisions about pieces of work. If you are not already reasonably familiar with the subject, turn up some long rods of different timbers, each about 50mm (2in) diameter. Divide them up into 100mm (4in) sections, and try a different finish on each section. Write what you are intending to do on the wood before you start.

N.B. *If the product is to be used for food or drink, the finish must be non-toxic. For drinking vessels, use products specifically designed for that particular job. For other vessels to be used for food, use teak or olive oil.*

FILLERS

While fillers are of less use to turners than to most other woodworkers, you should try to develop a basic knowledge of them. For small holes, rather than grain filling, the best filler is Beaumontage, a mixture of beeswax and resin that takes most finishes and can easily be stained to match surrounding timber. It can be useful for burr timbers where the temptation otherwise is to use a wax finish, and let the wax fill the holes. Generally speaking, the only time you will need to use fillers is on open grain woods, particularly ash, chestnut, walnut and mahogany. (Oak needs a different treatment, which I will cover separately.)

The surface to be filled should first be sanded smooth, two coats of thinned shellac applied in the normal manner and left to dry for at least a day. Slightly dampen a clean cotton cloth with a little water, dip it into some dental plaster, and then apply it to the wood on a slow lathe until the paste begins to turn slightly lumpy. Remove the excess immediately with a piece of dry hessian and, before it has chance to dry any further, clean the work using a fresh cotton cloth dampened with raw linseed oil. To stop the result looking rather streaky, add a little powdered water pigment of the appropriate colour to the dry plaster powder before applying. The result will be a firm base for the subsequent finish.

To fill oak, add a little French chalk to ordinary shellac, and then apply two or three coats of this mixture in the normal way, sanding lightly between coats.

There are many good commercial filler pastes available. These vary from country to country, and the best way to sort things out is to ask around locally to find out what other woodworkers in your area use.

ABRASIVES

There are two things in woodturning guaranteed to start an argument if more than one person is present. One is scraping, and the other is abrasives. All experienced turners agree on one thing: if you have a bad finish from the chisel, you cannot put it right with abrasive paper. This is where agreement ends. Some turners will not allow abrasives in their workshop, others swear by wire wool, others swear at wire wool, others use the wood shavings, others cloth-backed materials.

However you approach them, abrasives are for removing nibs (tiny imperfections) not flattening out great lumps left by poor turning. If your tools are sharp and your technique good, the need for abrasives is much reduced, but I believe that their use in finishing work is as necessary as it is in fine cabinet making. You should never use anything coarser than 180 grit for finishing.

For use between coats of varnish, abrasive paper at 320 or 400 grit is one option, while the wood shavings from the timber in question is another, or you could use 0000 wire wool. The opponents of wire wool say that it sticks in the timber and can discolour it, but as long as your preparation is good, this should not be a problem. Do not use wire wool on bare timber because you will never get the bits of wire out of the grain.

One word of warning: sanding bare timber on a lathe is one of the filthiest jobs there is. Dust gets everywhere. You must make sure that you have a sufficiently good dust extraction system to cope with it. Try to work out a way of attaching the hose of your extractor somewhere close to the work. This is of particular importance with those timbers that have irritant qualities, such as the rosewoods. For such materials, filter type face masks are the minimum requirement, but serious consideration should be given to face masks that can be plugged in to a dust extractor.

WAX

While many timbers are improved by waxing, the ones that benefit most tend to be those with an open texture such as ash, oak or chestnut. Many waxes produced for the do-it-yourself market have a high proportion of silicones in them. This gives them the advantage of producing a quick shine, but the shine is very much on the surface, and is usually short-lived.

The two main waxes for turnery are beeswax and carnauba, which are easy to obtain in their raw and prepared states. A good wax, properly applied, will last for years without further attention and will withstand a good deal of handling. Most suppliers of woodworking materials supply a wide range of waxes and it is essential that you check that the wax you are buying is appropriate to the purpose.

THE QUICK METHOD While the work is still spinning on the lathe, apply a thin coat of sanding sealer, and allow it to dry. This will take only about a minute. Rub the work down very lightly, and apply a coat of soft wax using a cotton cloth. Allow it to stand for about fifteen minutes before rubbing down with a cotton cloth, applying a second coat if required. This kind of finish will not stand a great deal of handling and will need to be attacked regularly with a can of polish.

COMPLETE WAXING The best wax to use for a long-lasting finish is one with a very high beeswax content, but the key to any good finish is preparation, and for wax this means first applying two coats of thinned shellac. Allow each to dry for 24 hours before sanding lightly. The best way to apply the wax is to use two layers of muslin, with the wax sandwiched between them. Squeeze this sack of wax gently, forcing a very thin layer on to the wood. The heat generated by the spinning timber will warm the wax and cause it to flow quite easily. Take care not to put on too thick a layer.

Then allow it to stand for at least an hour before polishing it with a piece of clean dry cloth. If the cloth fills up with the wax it removes, start a new piece. You have finished when you can stroke the surface without leaving a mark. Set it aside for a further day before applying the next coat. Depending on the timber, between four and six coats will be needed.

The exception to this method is walnut, which can look rather insipid if not specially prepared. Before putting the shellac on, give it a thin coat of raw linseed oil and leave it to stand for a couple of days before doing any further work. To check whether it is ready, rub the work with the back of your hand; if any oil gets on to your skin, give it another day. Once it is fully dry, apply the shellac and wax as above.

OIL

Many people recommend oiling as the easiest form of finish for timber. I really cannot go along with this, except to agree that there is, as with wax, a quick version of oiling sufficient to convince most people. Properly done however, it is the most time consuming of all finishes. The benefit is that when it is done, it imparts the most beautiful glow, which comes from deep within the timber. It also renders the timber reasonably impervious to heat and water, and it will never show patches caused by wear or small chips. A proper oiling is the nearest thing there is to a universal finish.

I have two reservations, however. The first is that to the untutored eye, the finish can look like a dull varnish, and secondly, it is very time consuming. Unless your products are destined for places where quality is sufficiently highly valued, such as your own house, a full oil finish may be commercially inappropriate.

THE QUICK METHOD Frankly, all you do is get the wood spinning on the lathe and rub an oily cloth over it once a day for three days. There are a wide variety of brand named oils with similar sounding names, all having totally different formulations. You have to shop around your own suppliers and try out as many as you can, picking out those you prefer. Alternatively, you can make up your own mixture of one part turpentine, one part waterproof varnish and two parts linseed oil. Do not show the product in discriminating company, but it is quite acceptable for the mass market.

COMPLETE OILING As applying oil properly requires a great deal of hard rubbing, it makes sense to use a lathe so the wood does all the work. The idea is not to get the timber covered in oil and wait for it to soak in; if you try this you will find an unpleasant residue

appears on the surface. The object is to let the oil grow warm with the friction, and work its way into the wood, so that the finish is genuinely part of the material, not something extra added on as an afterthought.

There is only one kind of oil to use, raw linseed. There are a number of products on the market containing the oil plus 'improvers'. These extras are designed to reduce the time it takes to do the job, but at some expense to the finished article. The only acceptable additive is one part turpentine to two parts oil, a mixture used commercially to reduce the time needed between coats.

The method is simple. Before you set the work spinning on the lathe, brush on enough oil to cover the work with a fine layer all over, then run the lathe at the highest speed compatible with the size of piece, and polish it with a very soft cotton cloth. When the oil has disappeared, which will take a few minutes, set the work on one side for several days. The second coat should not be applied until the work can be handled without getting any traces of oil on your hands. Depending on the temperature and humidity, this will take from three to seven days. It will take a coat a week for a month to produce an adequate finish, and a coat a month for the next year to produce a spectacular finish.

N.B. If you are oiling a thin piece of work, both sides must be treated, otherwise the uneven absorption of oil will cause the piece to split.

VARNISH

This is an impossible area to deal with briefly, since there are hundreds of different varnishes on the market, all with the instructions on the tin. The best advice is for you to try a few out and see which you prefer. Of the varnishes on the market, only choose ones targeted at woodturners, which are widely available through woodworking magazines or from suppliers of woodturning materials, and are usually good at their job.

To be somewhat judgemental about it, varnishes may be the easy option, but I do not like finishes that sit on the surface and gleam at you so brightly that you cannot see the timber underneath. The other drawback is that they will quickly show signs of wear on objects that come in for a lot of handling. Nevertheless, they are useful, particularly when cost is a factor in the equation.

One specialized varnish with which you should be

familiar is the melamine type, used for vases and other vessels that are to be constantly filled with water. Once again, the various brands all do the job perfectly well, and the instructions on the tin are good. There are other varnishes available that are either furniture or outdoor types, and are not generally used on stand-alone turnery. If you do much in the way of furniture repair or garden ornaments, you do need to be familiar with them.

RECIPES

When heating the following solutions, use a double boiler, take care with ventilation, and do not get a naked flame anywhere near the solution.

1. Quick varnish/oil mixture. One part waterproof varnish (or spar varnish), one part turpentine, two parts raw linseed oil.

2. Hard oil. Using a double boiler, dissolve 25g of beeswax in 500ml of raw linseed oil, then add 500ml of turpentine.

3. Beeswax polish. Dissolve 500g of beeswax in 250ml of turpentine in a double boiler.

4. Carnauba polish. Melt 250g each of carnauba and ceresin wax in a double boiler, and add 250ml of turpentine to the resulting solution.

5. Soft wax. Using a double boiler, melt together one part carnauba wax, two parts ceresin wax and four parts paraffin wax. Add 500ml of turpentine for each kilo of wax to the resulting solution.

PART II

THE SHAPES

REVISING SHAPES AND SIZES

USING THE GRIDS

Rarely, if ever, does the design you have fit the piece of wood you have bought, and it becomes necessary either to waste timber or change the size of the planned object. You may simply want to make it larger or smaller, but you may wish to keep the height the same, making it thinner. All the objects in this book have been drawn to a few basic sizes, and you will certainly need to know how to change things. The process is actually fairly simple.

All the drawings in the book have been printed on a grid. To increase or decrease the size, draw a second grid on a piece of thin card, then follow the line of the original drawing and each time it crosses a line on the printed grid, mark the same point on your grid. By the time you have finished you will have a couple of dozen points on your grid, which you simply join up. Since none of them are very far apart, this is not difficult. Life may be a little easier if you have a set of French curves for this, but it is not really necessary.

EXAMPLES The size of your grid is worked out according to the amount by which you wish to increase or decrease the original drawing. In a simple case, if you wish to double the size of the object, you make the squares on your grid twice the size of the one in the book. Similarly, if you wish to make it half the size, you make your squares half the size.

Changing the size of a piece is a simple enough operation, but it is quite common to find that the new size is not as pleasing in its proportions as the original. The grid method can be used to change the proportions. If you like the original shape but think that the height is wrong for the diameter, you can change the height but not the diameter, or change the diameter, keeping the height the same.

If you wish to double the height of an object from the book, but only increase its diameter by one half, make your new grid in those proportions, i.e. no longer square, but oblong, twice as high but only one and a half times the width. To make an object wider without changing the height, once again, make your own grid oblong, but this time the same height as the grid in the book, but wider.

This grid method can be used to make very subtle changes, such as I had to do with a big oak chess set I made for outdoor use. None of the pieces have exactly the same proportions as the original Staunton design. Before you go to the lathe, make a cardboard cutout of the revised shape and stand back and look at it for a while before wasting time and timber. This is especially important if you are making a set of things to go together because you may find that the proportional changes you make to one piece are not the same as you make to another. In fact, I had to make different changes to each of the chess pieces when I changed from the standard size to giant, and again when I made a miniature set.

MULTIPLE TURNINGS

There are a certain number of tricks you can employ if you wish to make a number of identical items, of which the three main ones are the template, the scratch bar and the caliper setting jig.

The template is straightforward. In a piece of softwood, about a quarter of an inch thick, cut the profile of the object to be turned. This is held against the work as it nears its end to make sure that the curves are correct. You may be surprised at how little deviation is needed in the shape of a piece to make it look out of place amongst those it is supposed to match.

The scratch bar is a piece of wood into which a number of sharp pins have been fitted, points out. The bar matches the template, in that each pin is at a key point on the turning. Once the piece of timber has been turned to a round, the scratch bar is held against the work, marking the main parts of the finished object without the need for constant measuring, or even stopping the lathe.

The final object is the caliper setting jig. On a complicated piece of work there may be anything up to a dozen important diameters. To set the calipers with a measure each time is time consuming and can be inaccurate. If you cut a piece of softwood plank in steps, each step representing a different diameter, you can fix this somewhere on the bed of your lathe and set the calipers from it. Write the measurement involved by each step and write the diameters on the appropriate part of the template.

HOW THE SHAPES ARE ORGANIZED

I have divided the shapes into a number of convenient categories, but that does not mean to say that these divisions are rigid. If you see a shape in the goblet section that you think would make a good vase or egg cup, that is as it should be.

With lidded objects, I have indicated how I suggest the two parts should be fitted together, e.g. whether the lid should fit outside the base or have a foot that fits inside. However, with some objects, such as the fruit shaped pots, the continuity of the shape between the top and bottom is the most important feature. I have therefore drawn these with the lid in place, indicating the join with a dotted line. Whether the top fits in the bottom or visa versa is up to you.

A few objects, such as the teapots and jugs, have a handle on one side and a spout on the other. I have continued to draw only half the shape, drawing the variation of the other side using a dotted line.

Some items require a small amount of carving to be done, such as a jug. To make these, first turn the jug following the shape of the spout on the outside, and the shape of the smallest internal diameter on the inside. Then remove the item from the lathe and finish the top by carving it to shape.

N.B. The teapots, coffee pots, jugs, and cups and saucers are decorative items only, and should not be used for any practical purpose.

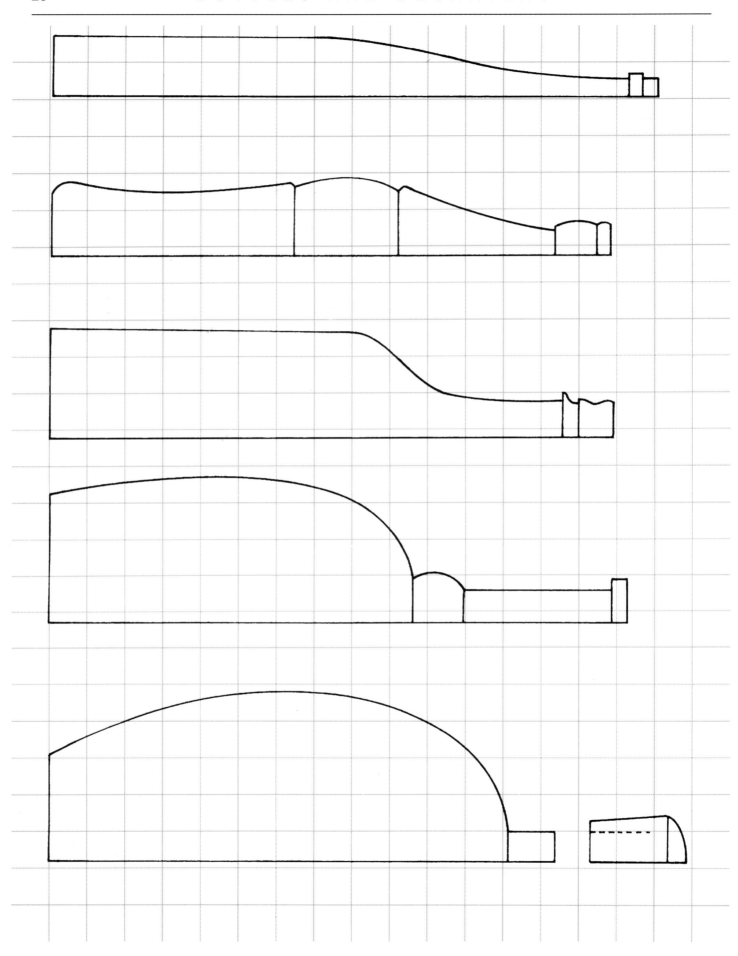

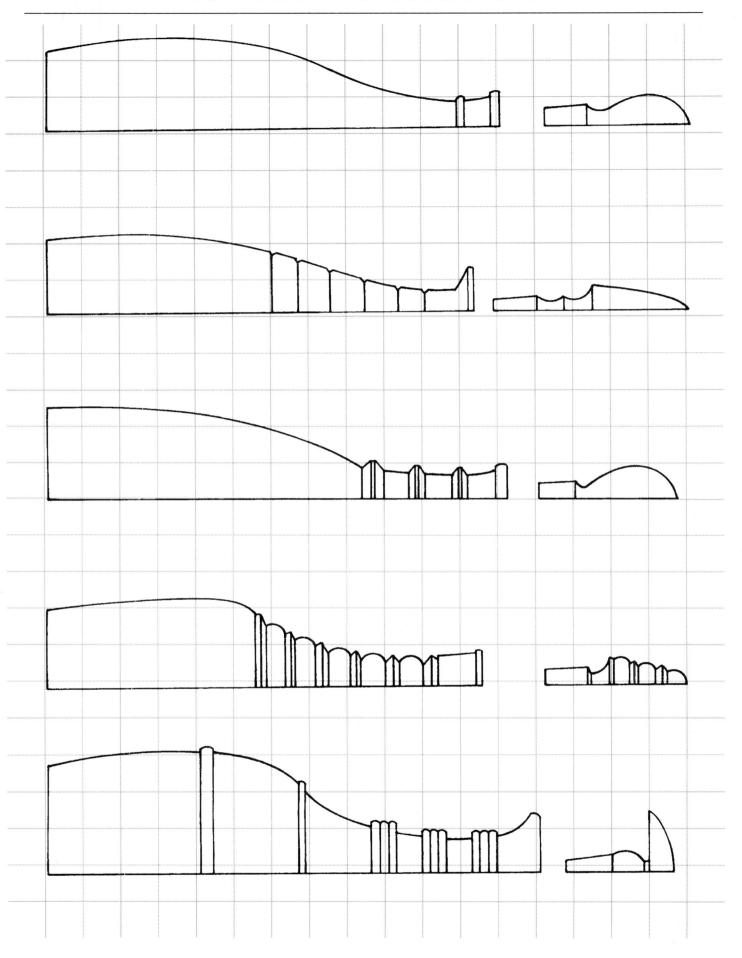

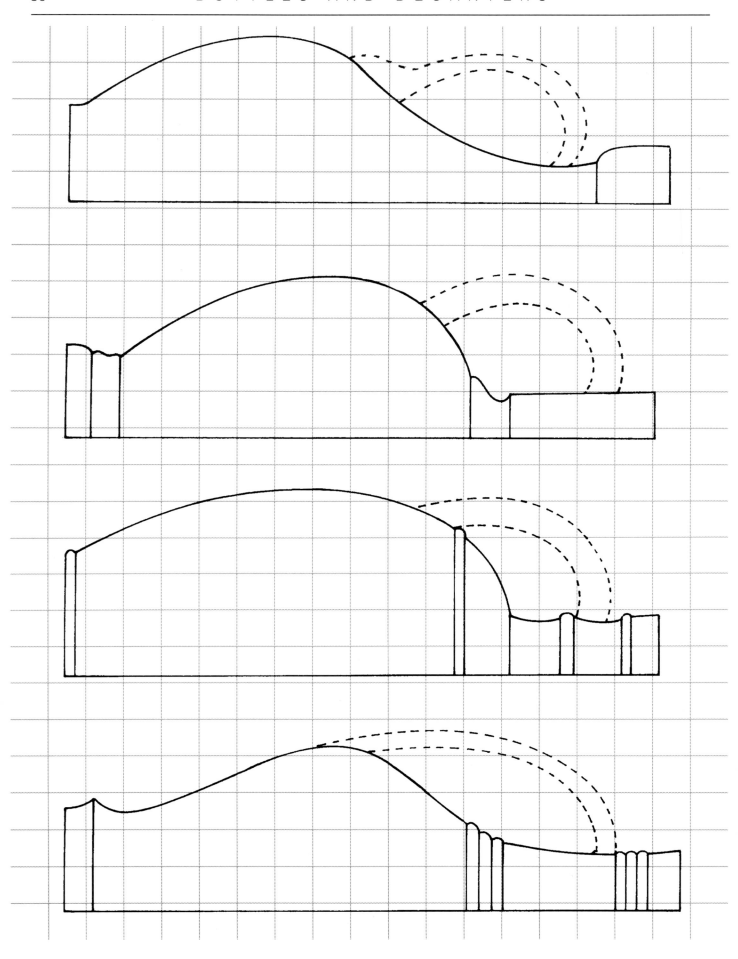

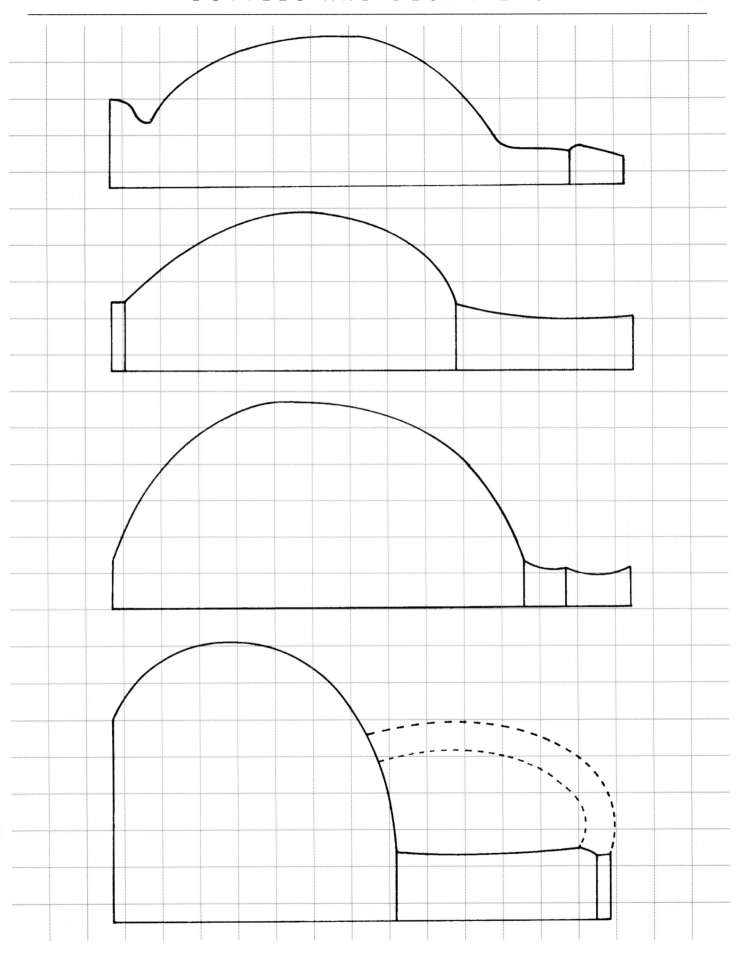

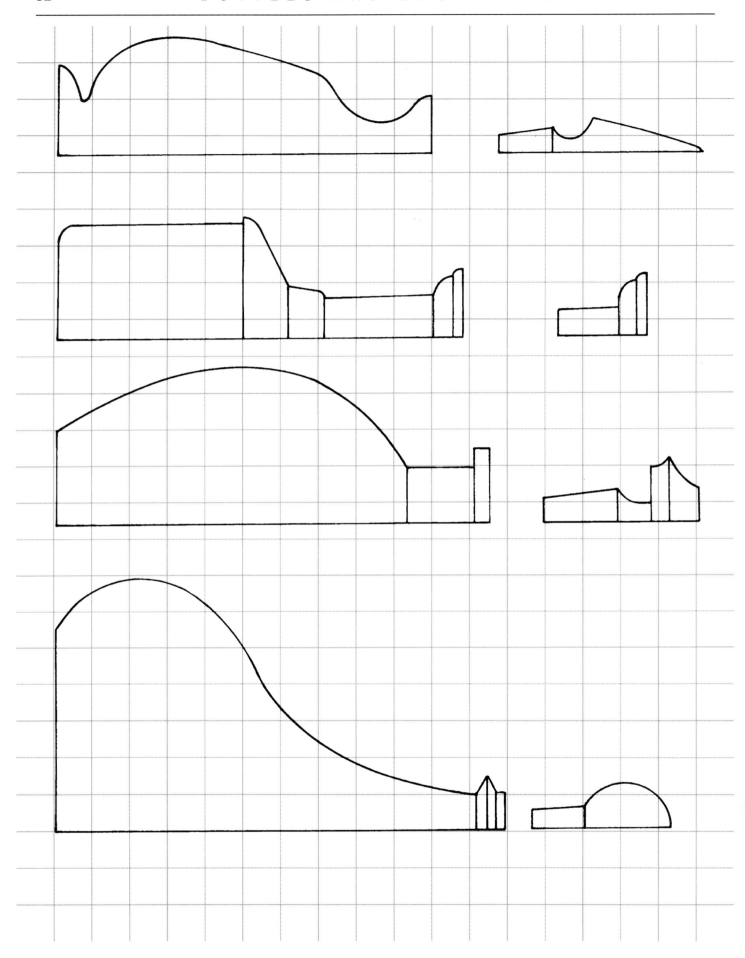

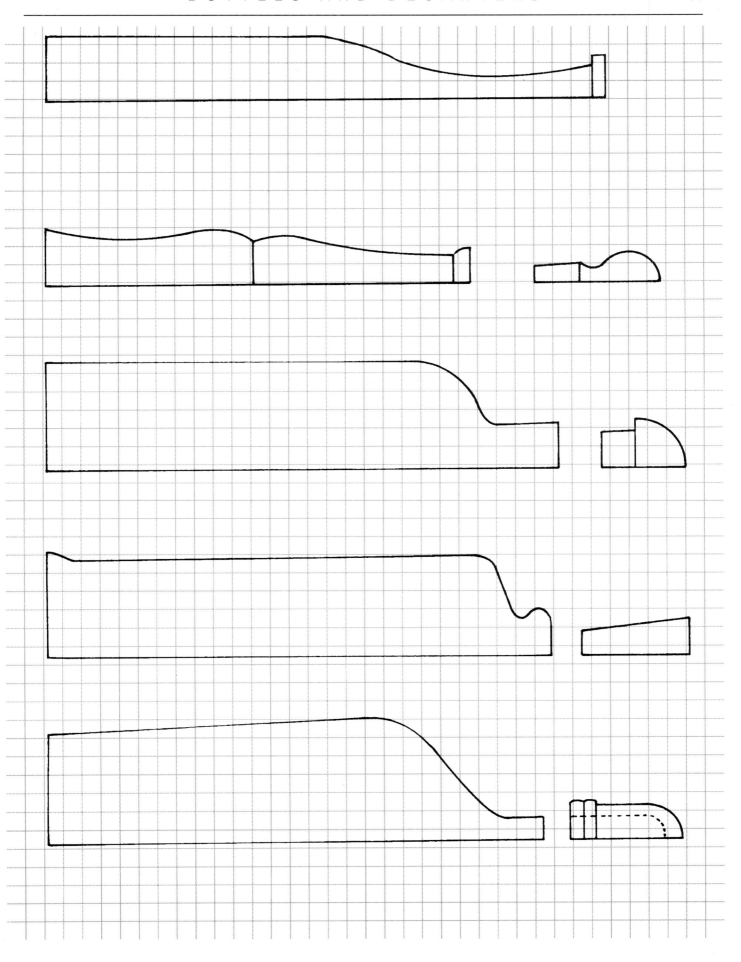

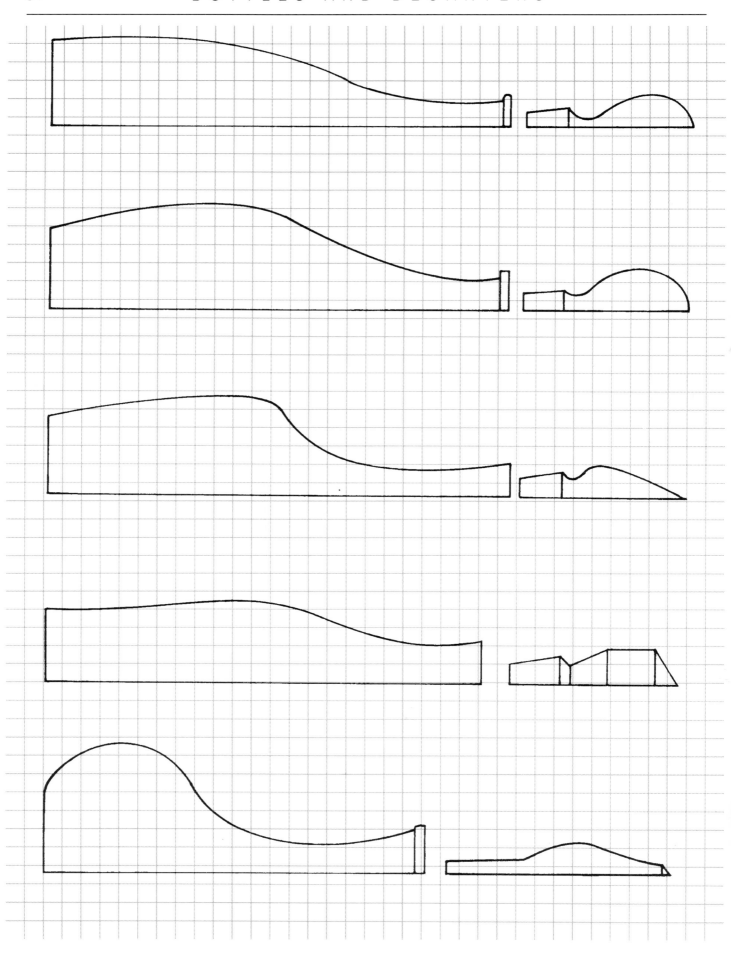

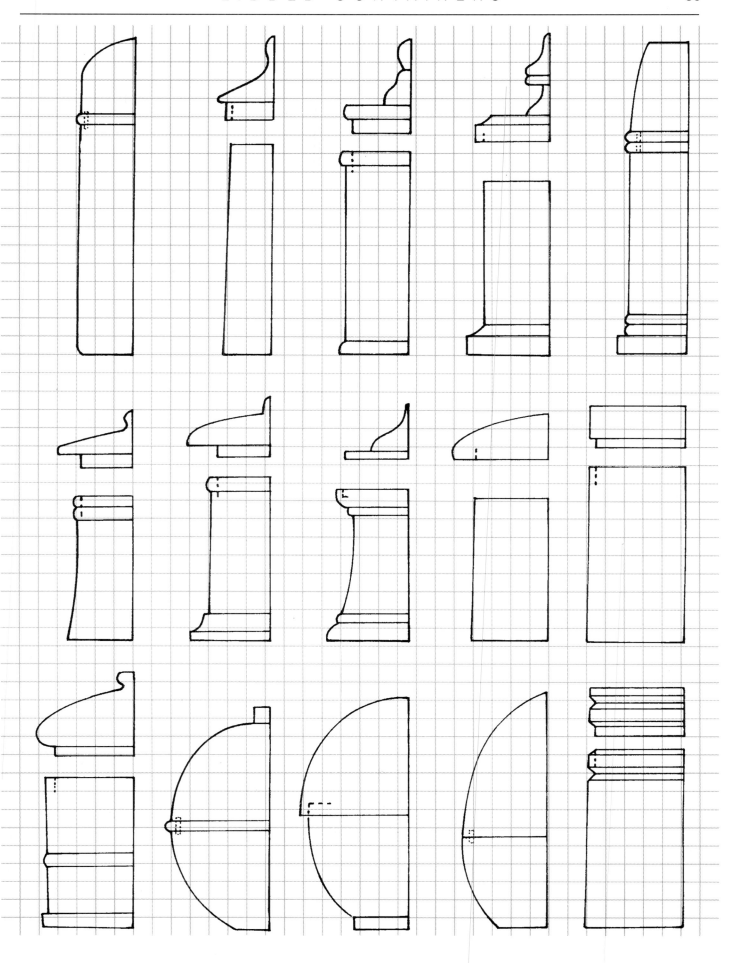

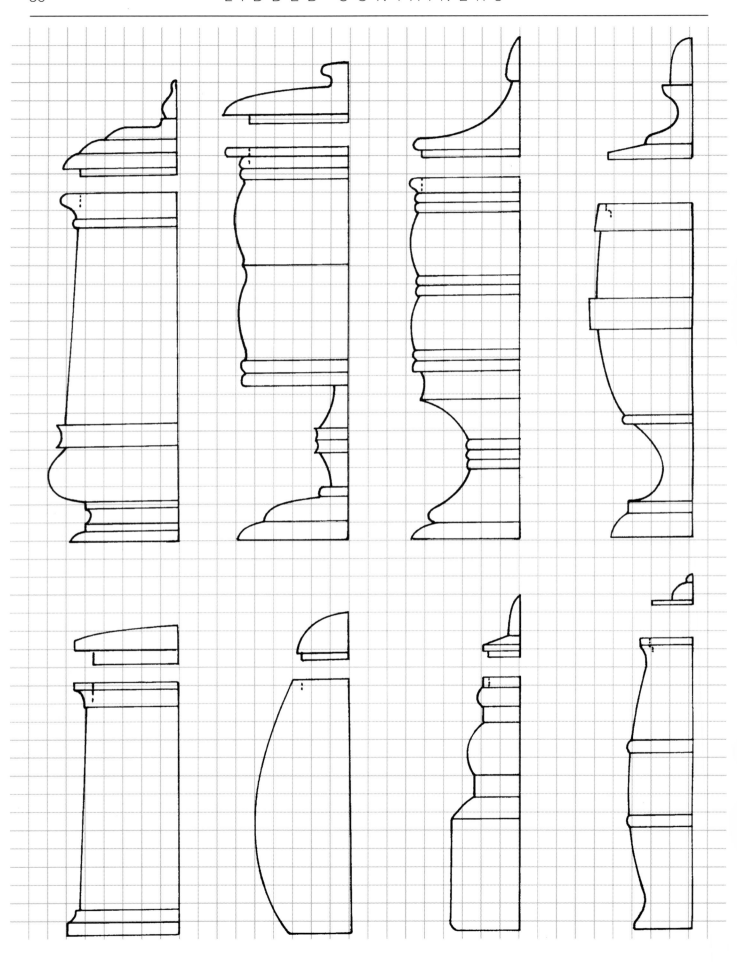

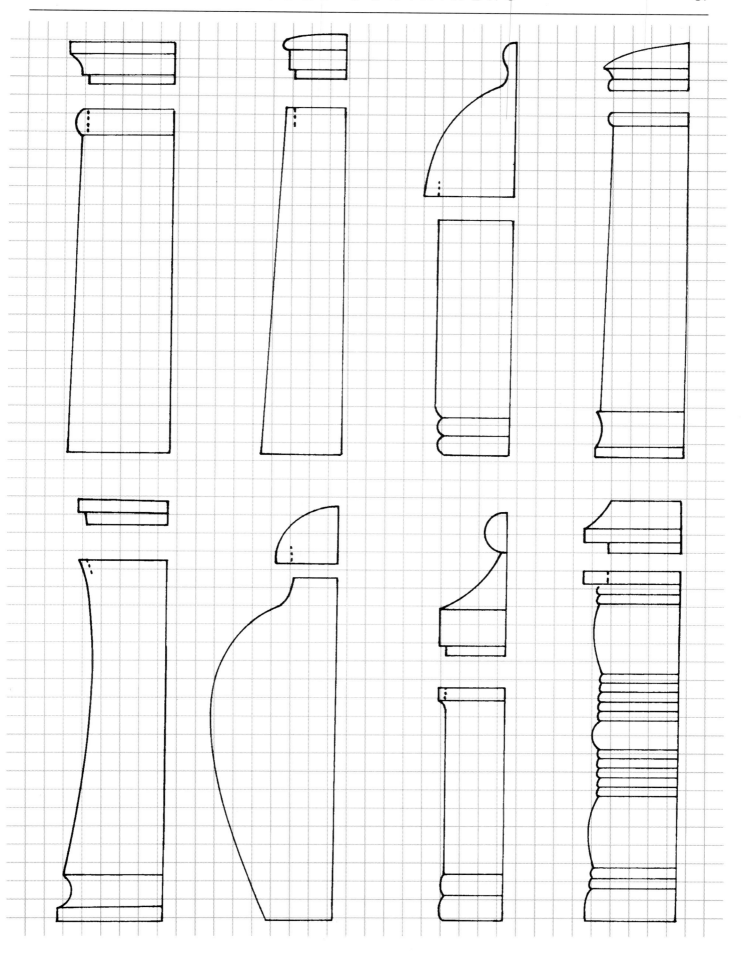

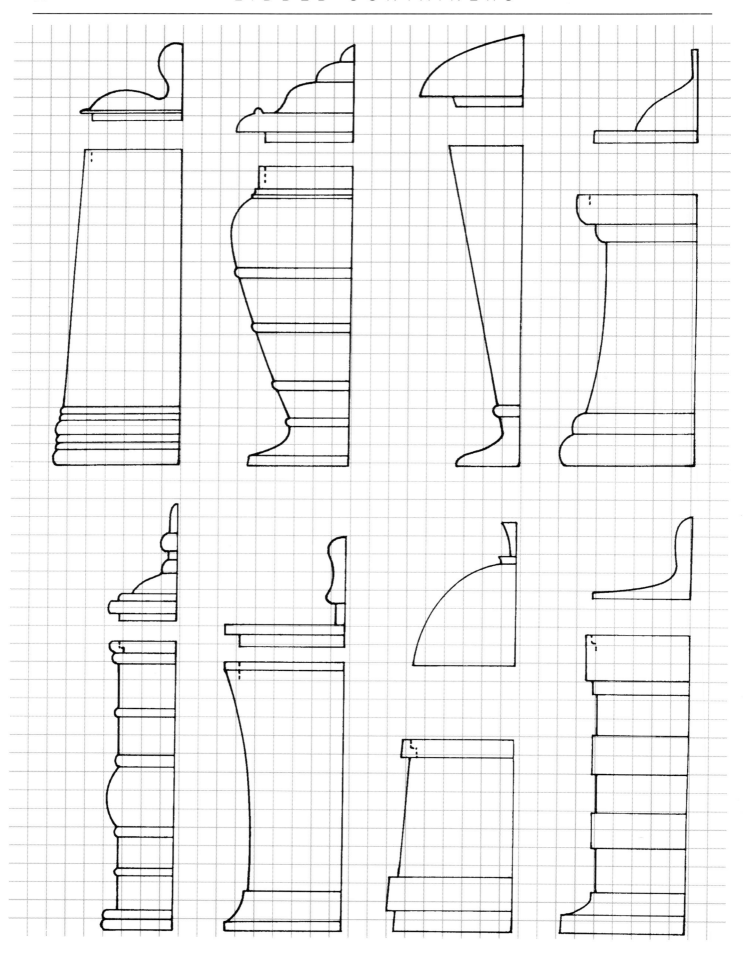

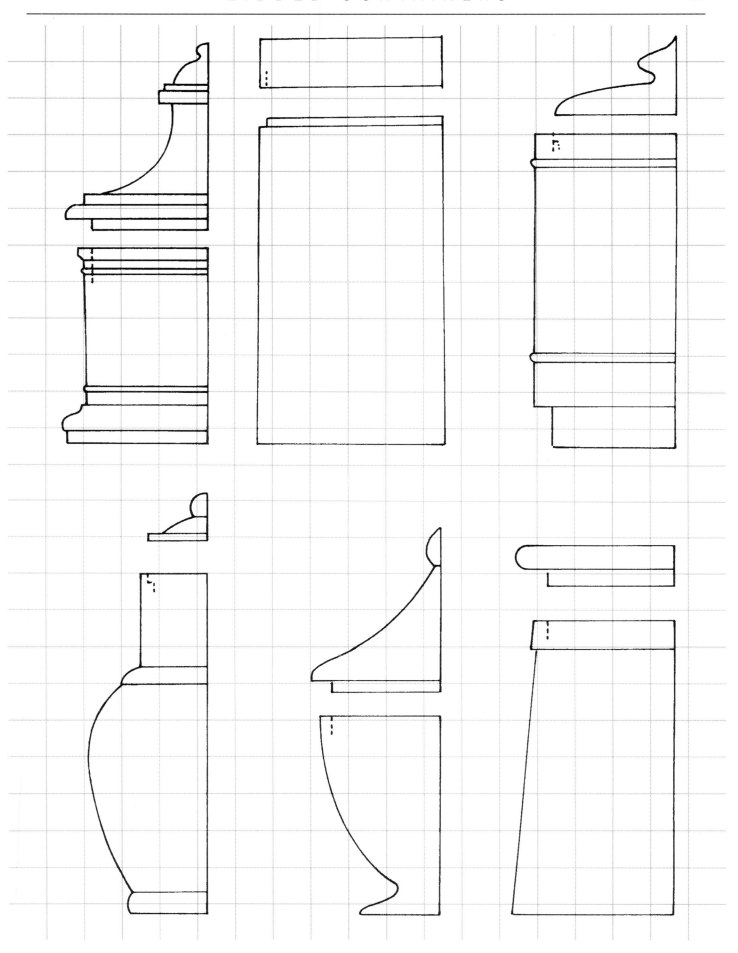

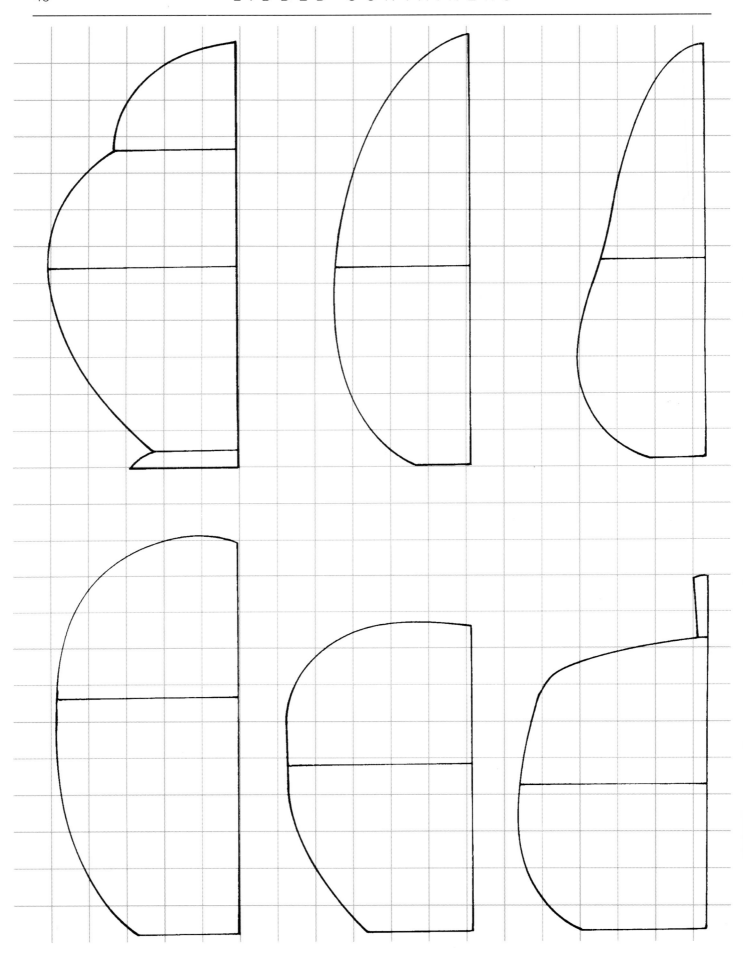

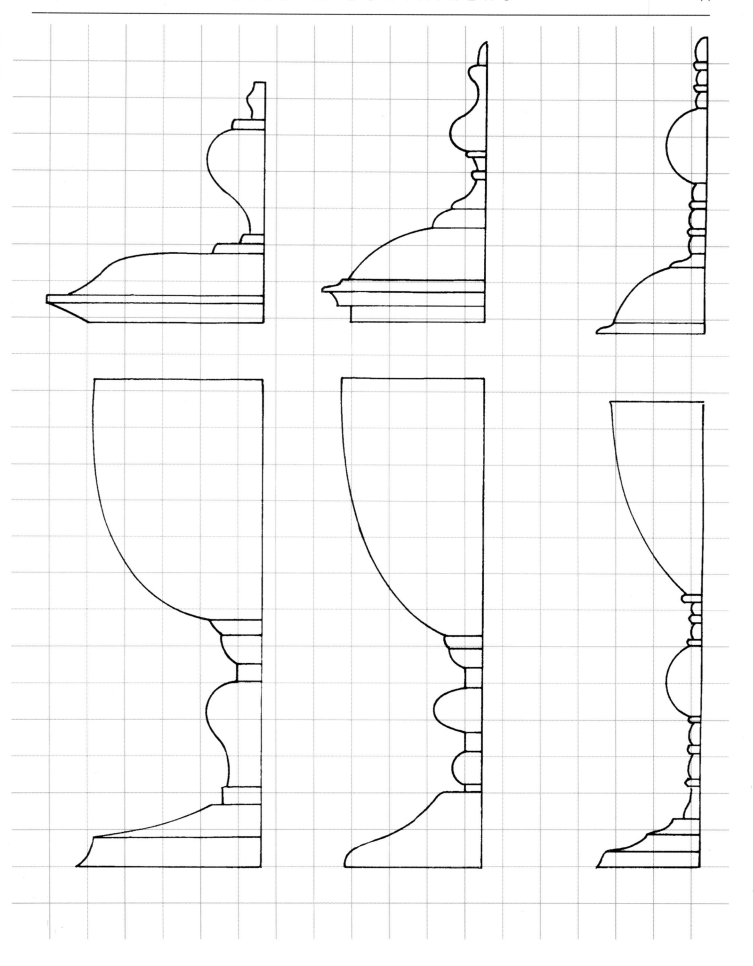

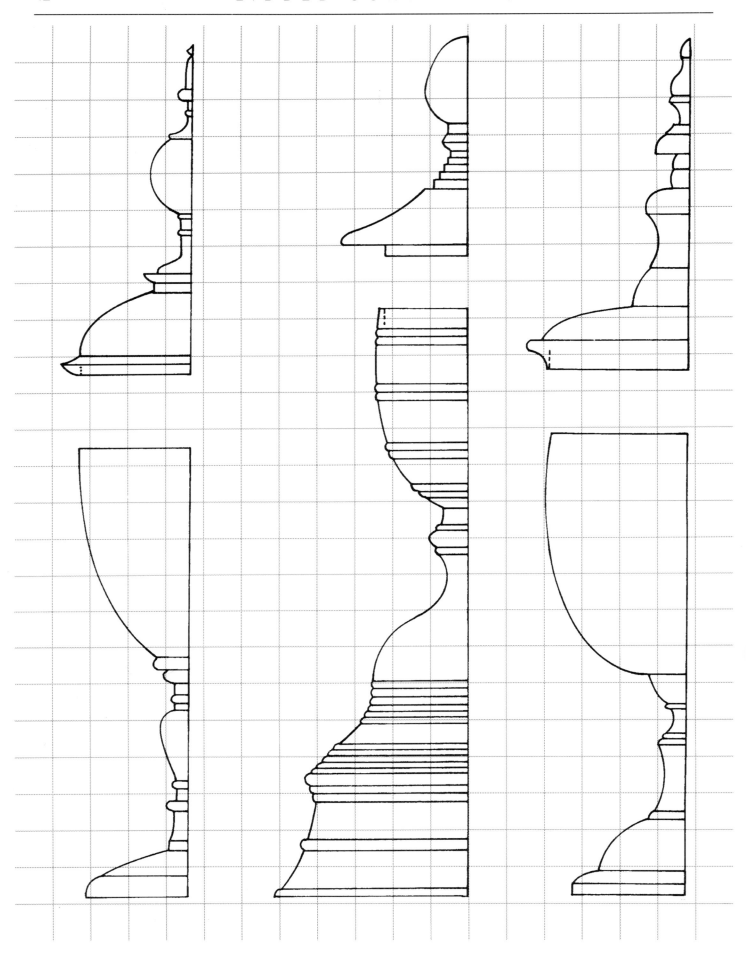

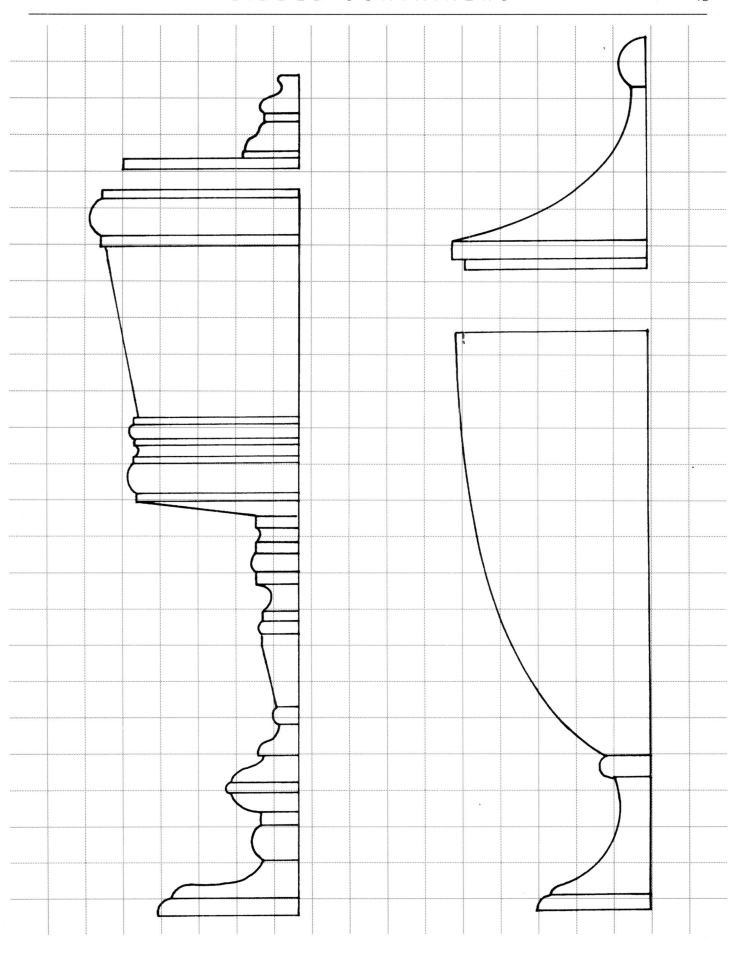

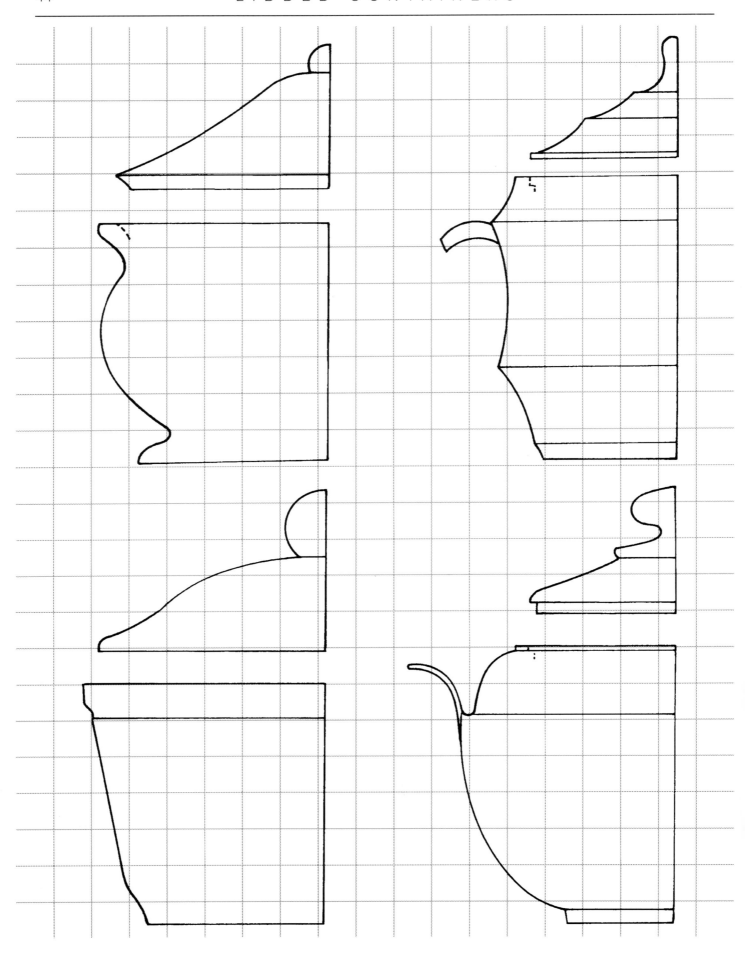

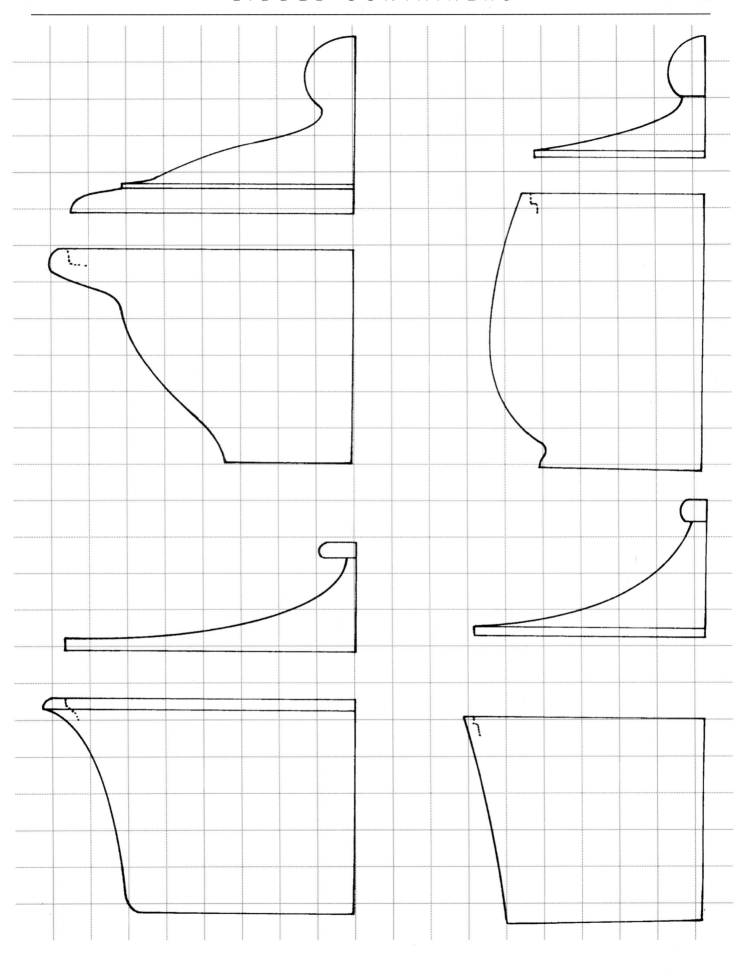

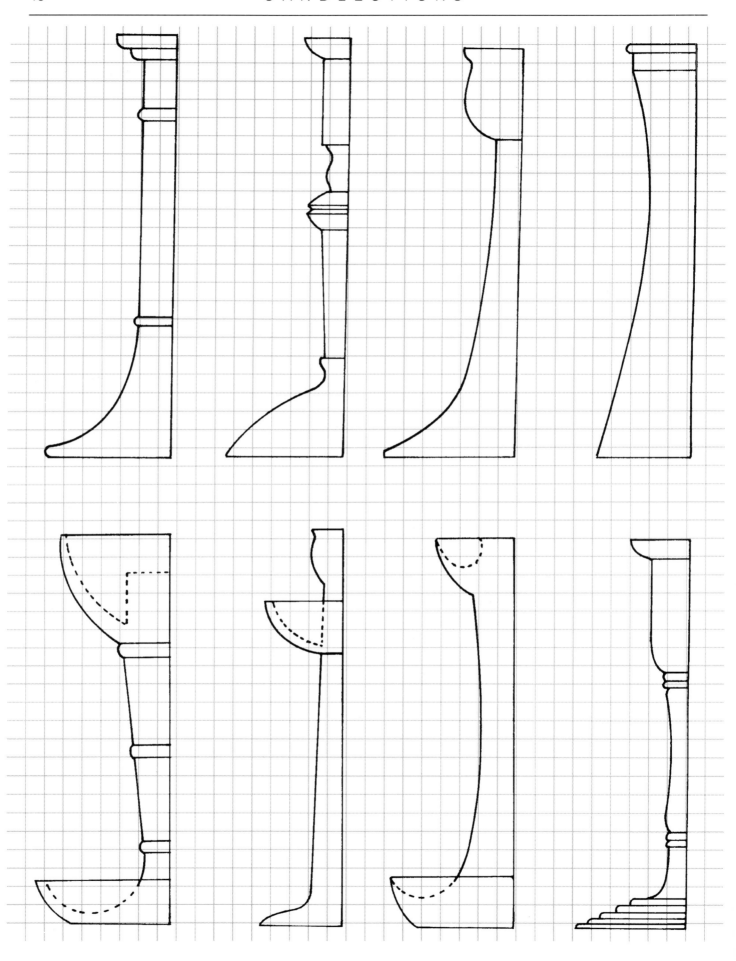

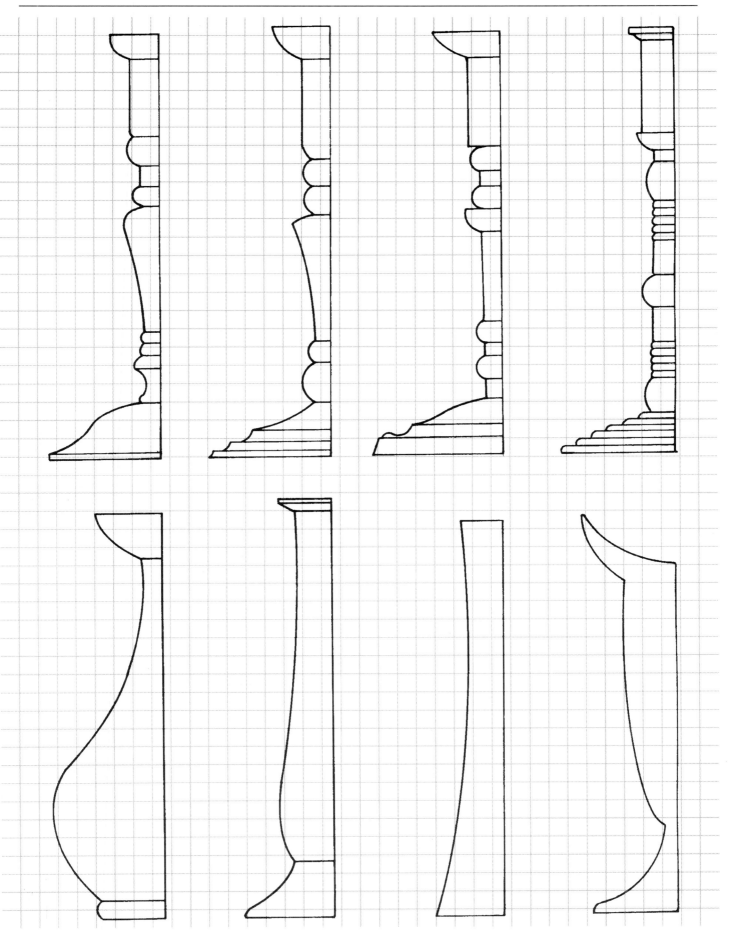

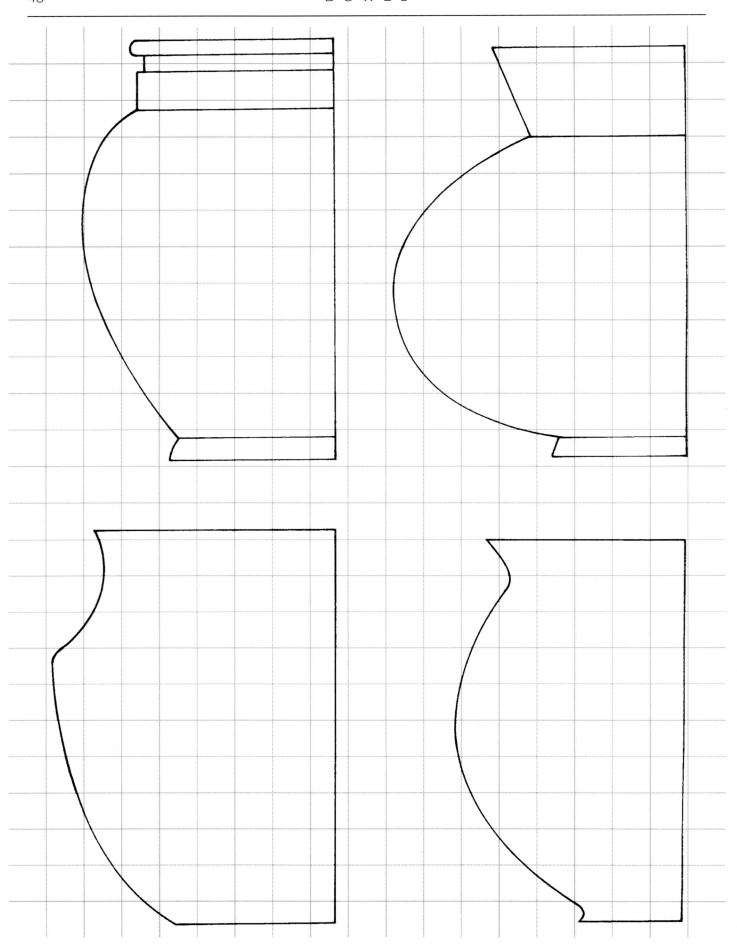

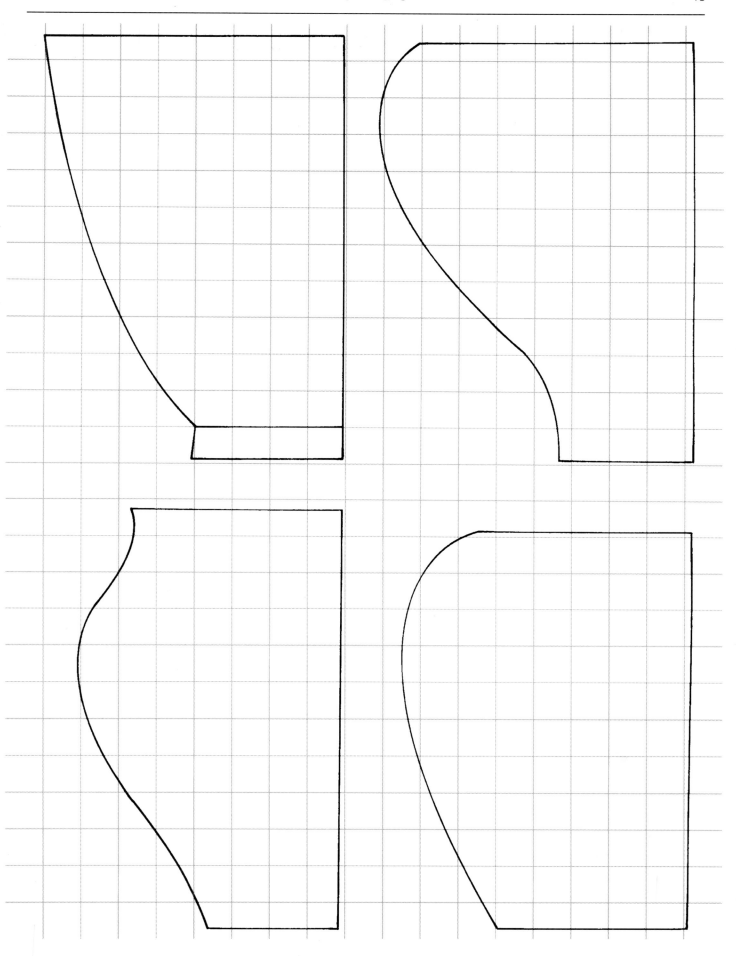

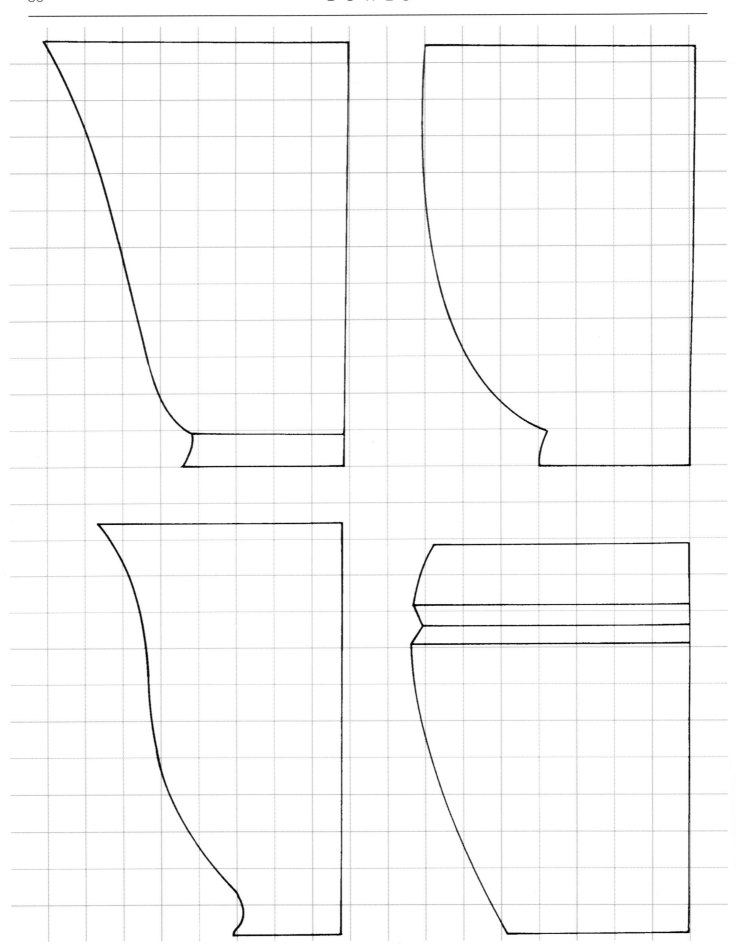

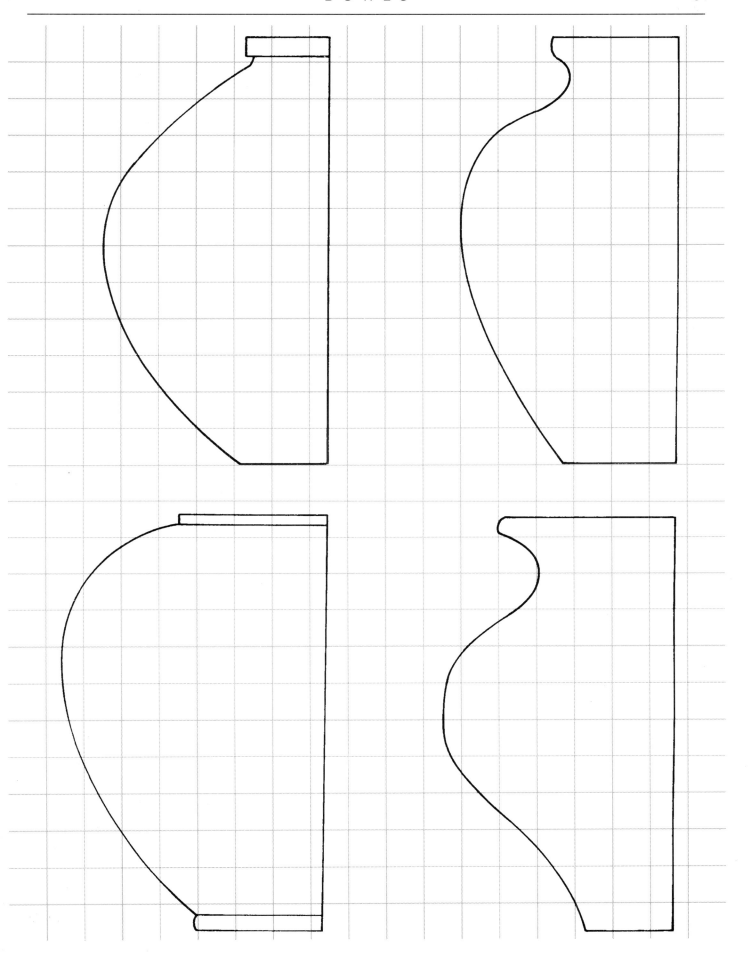

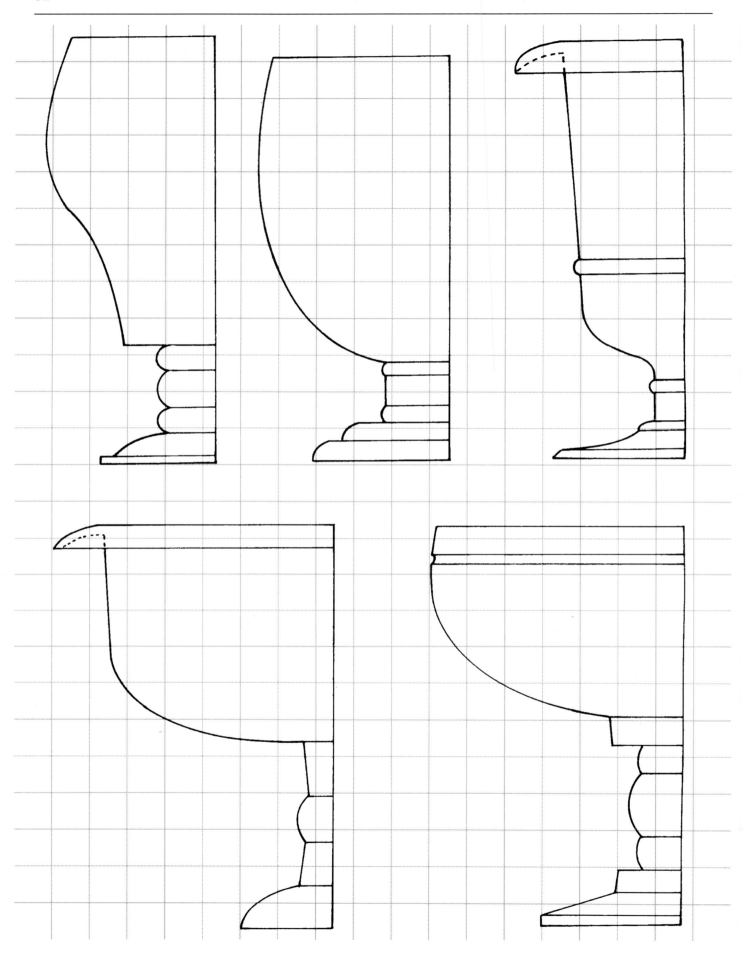

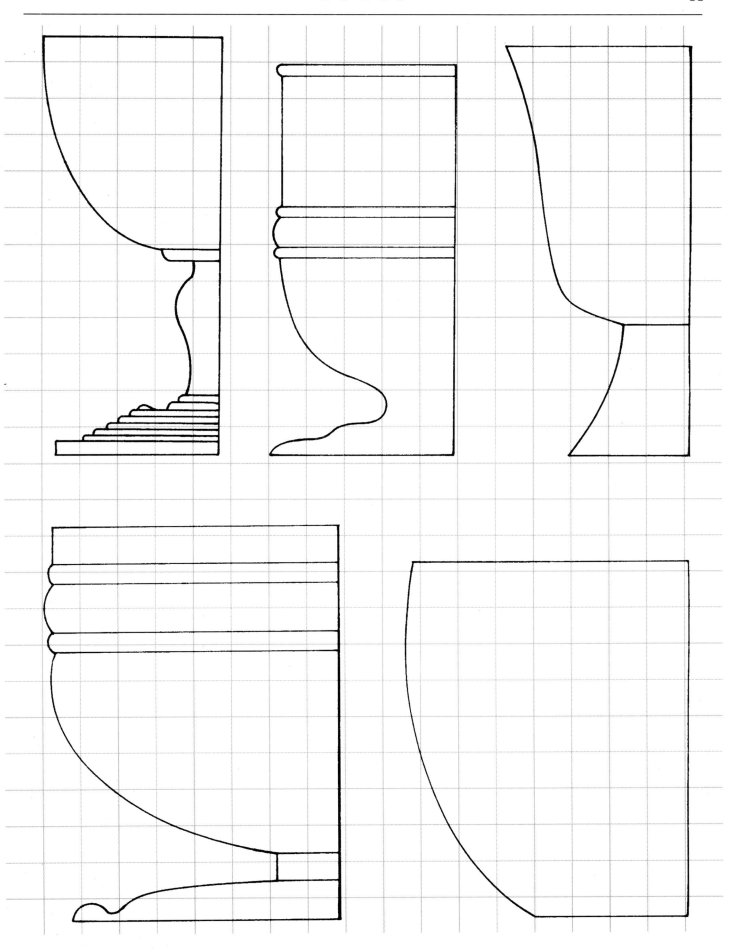

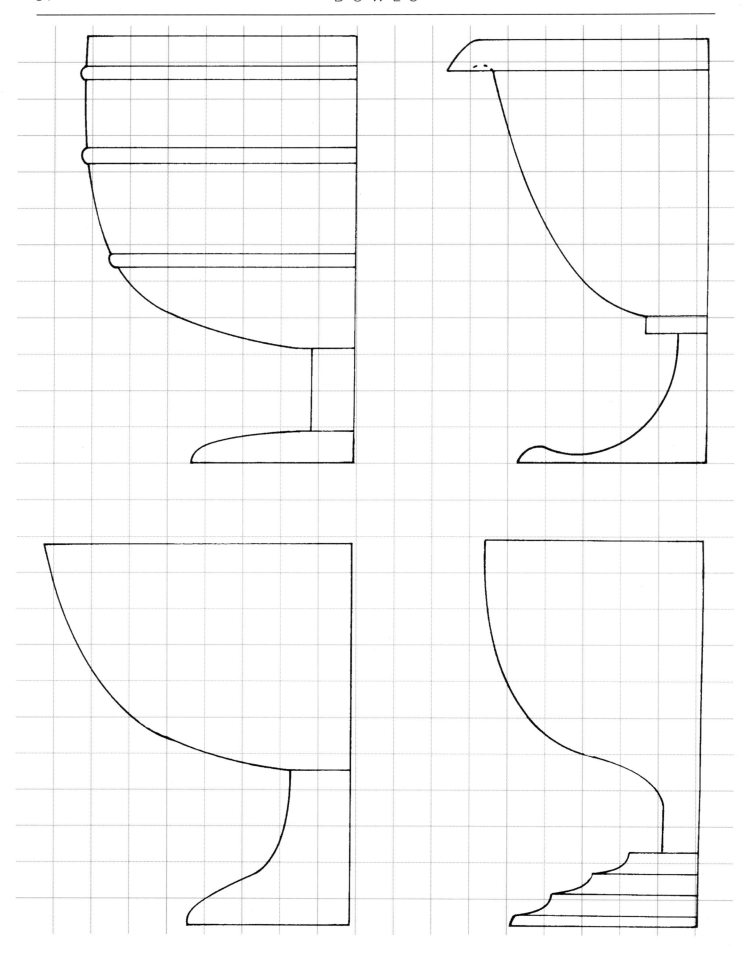

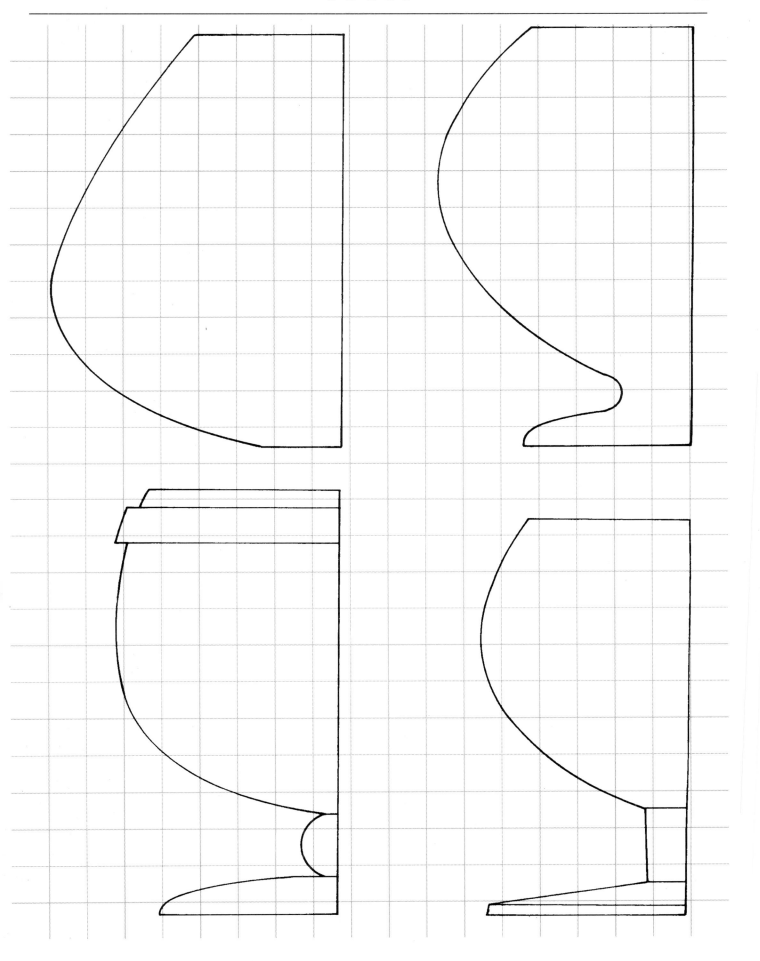

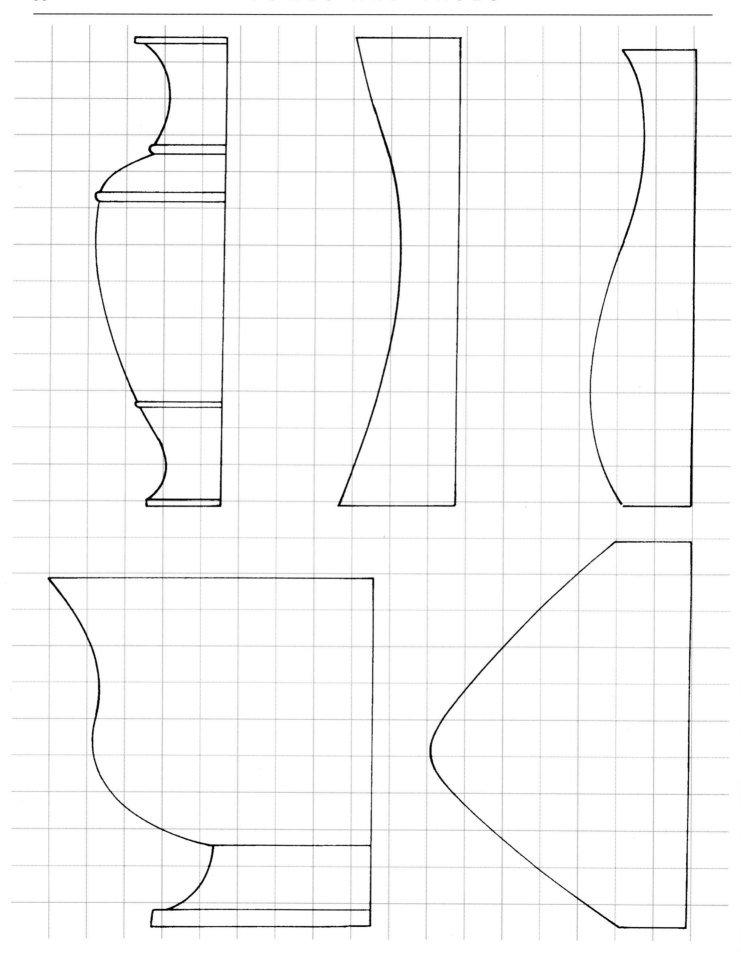

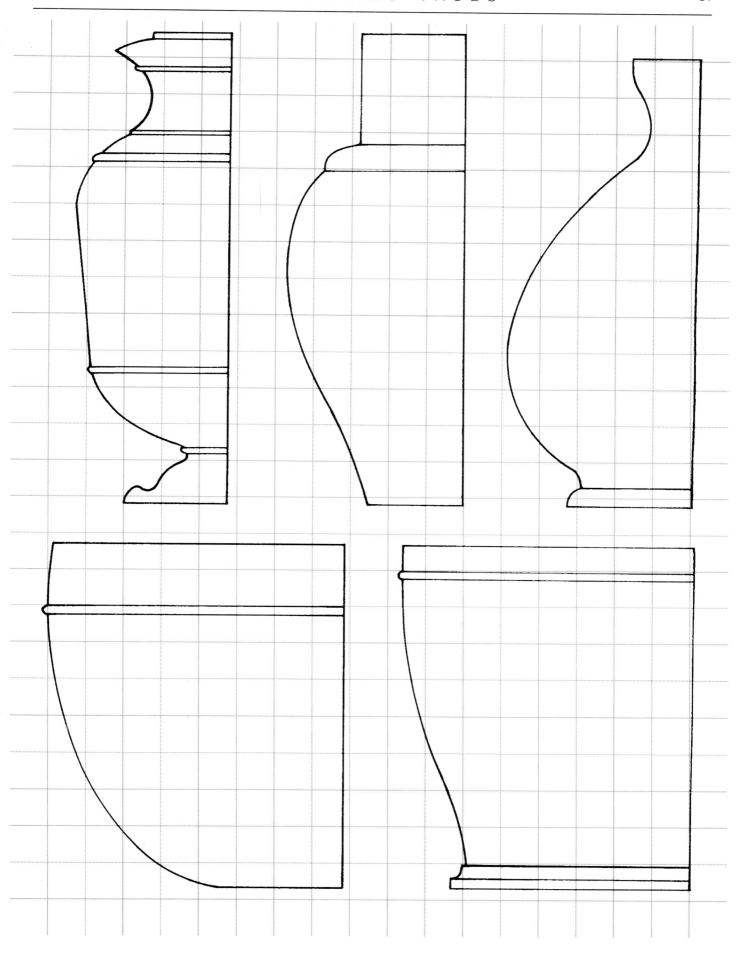

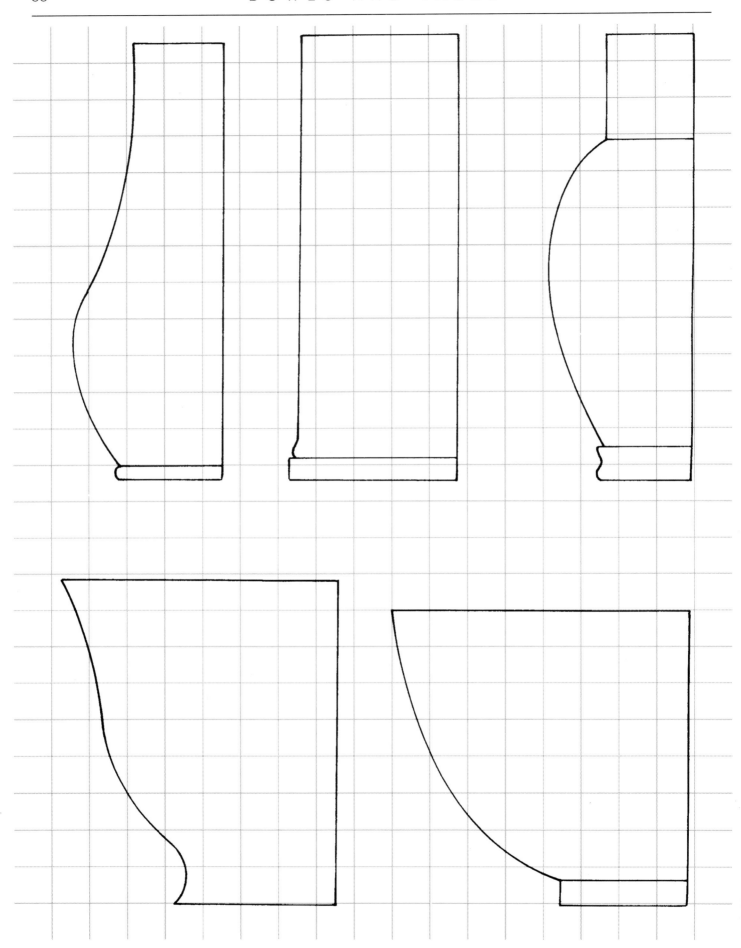

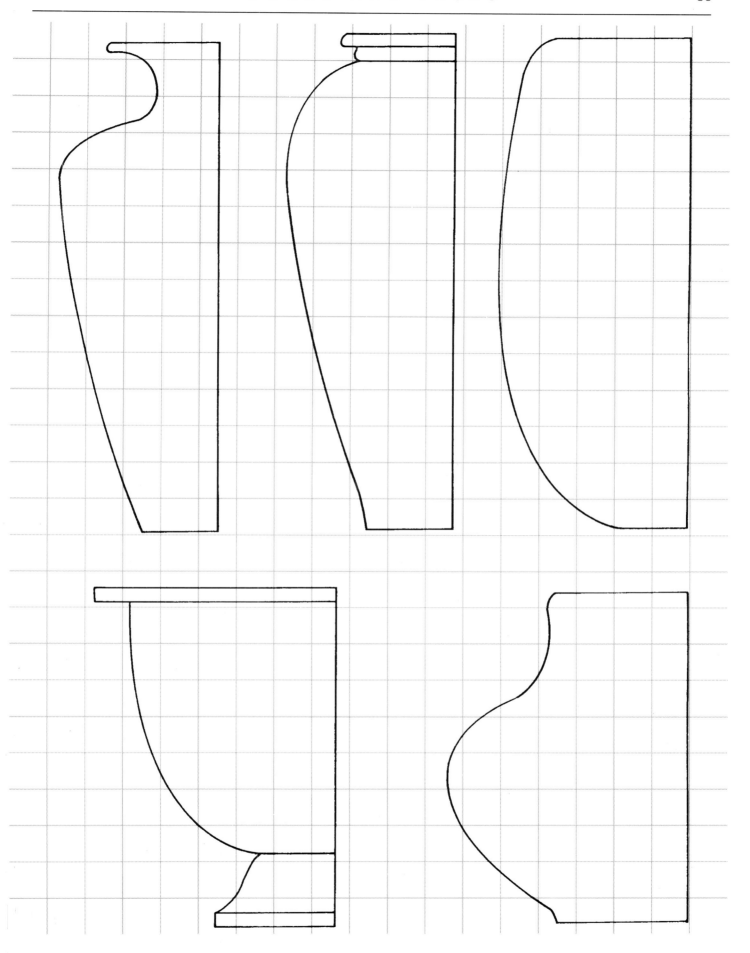

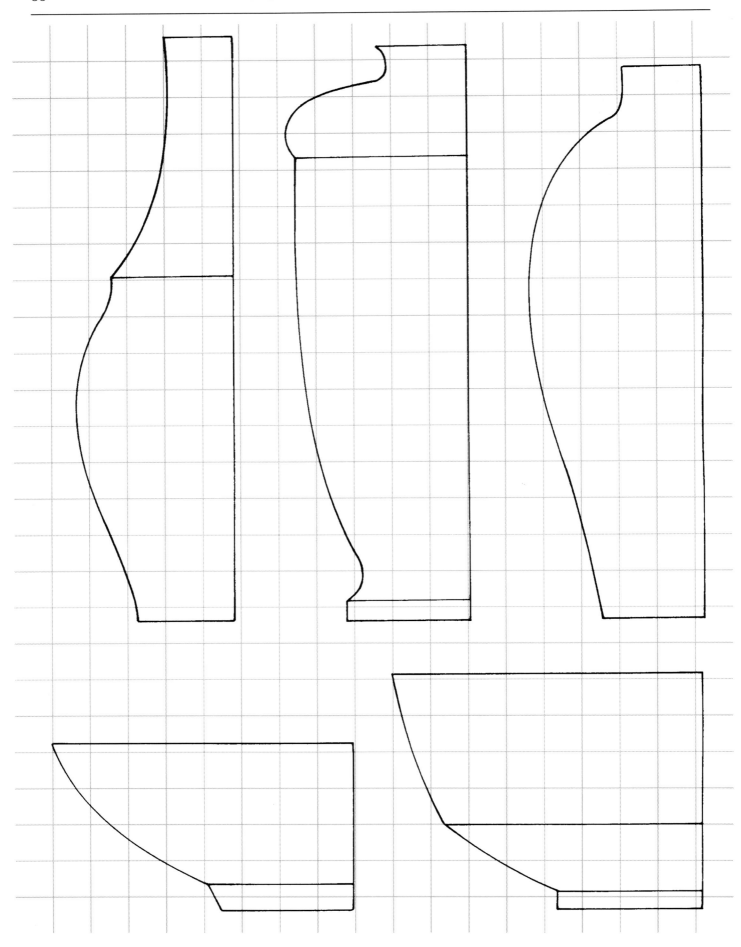

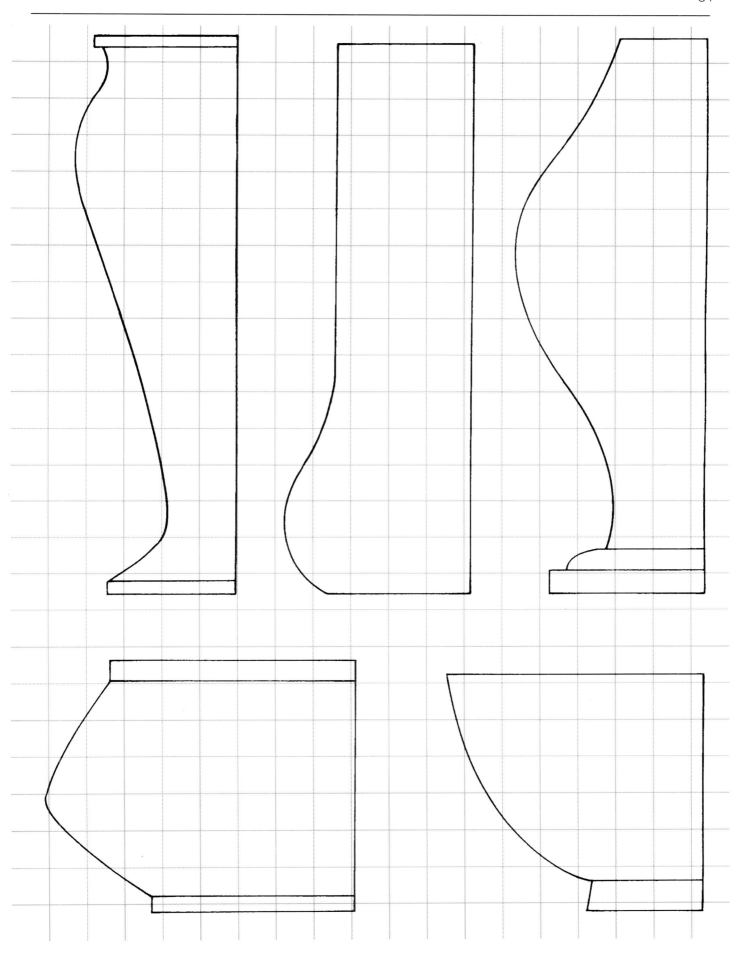

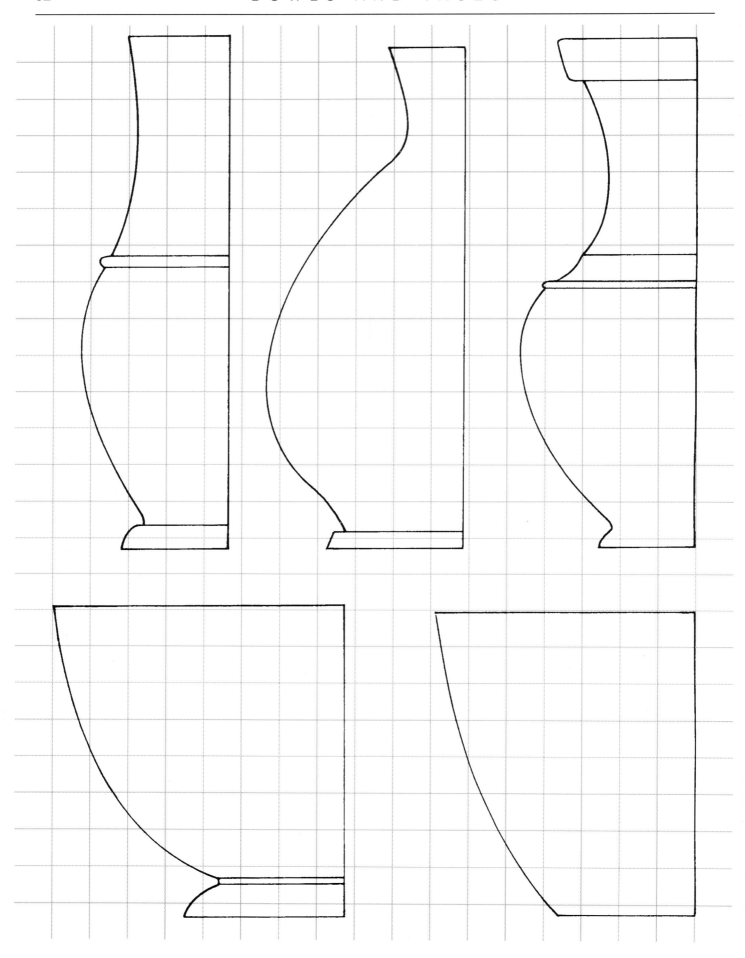

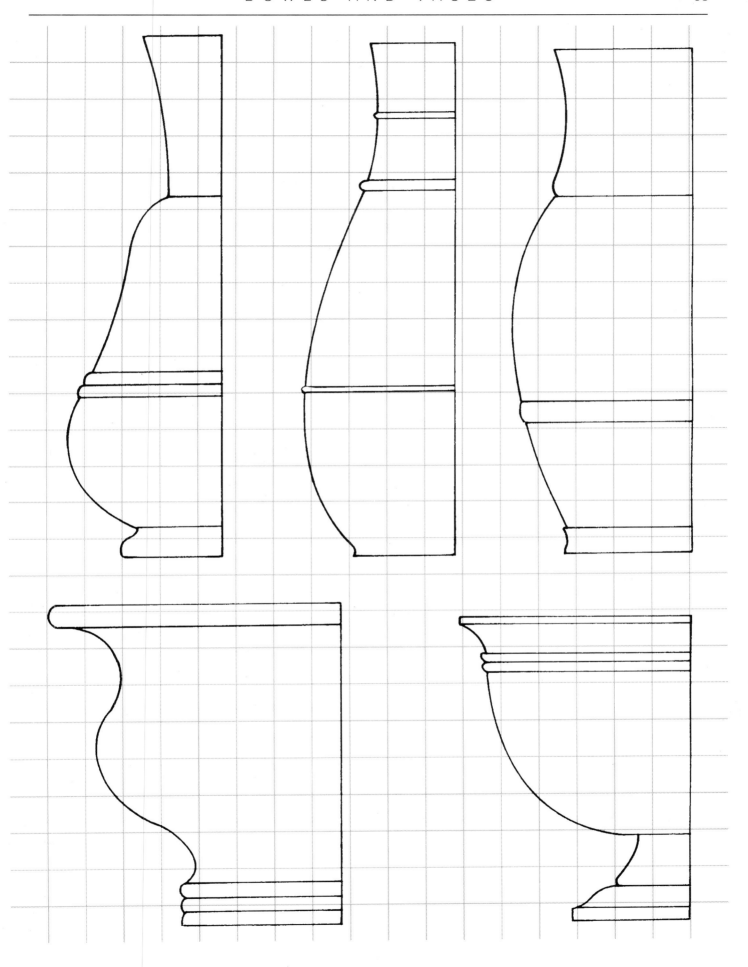

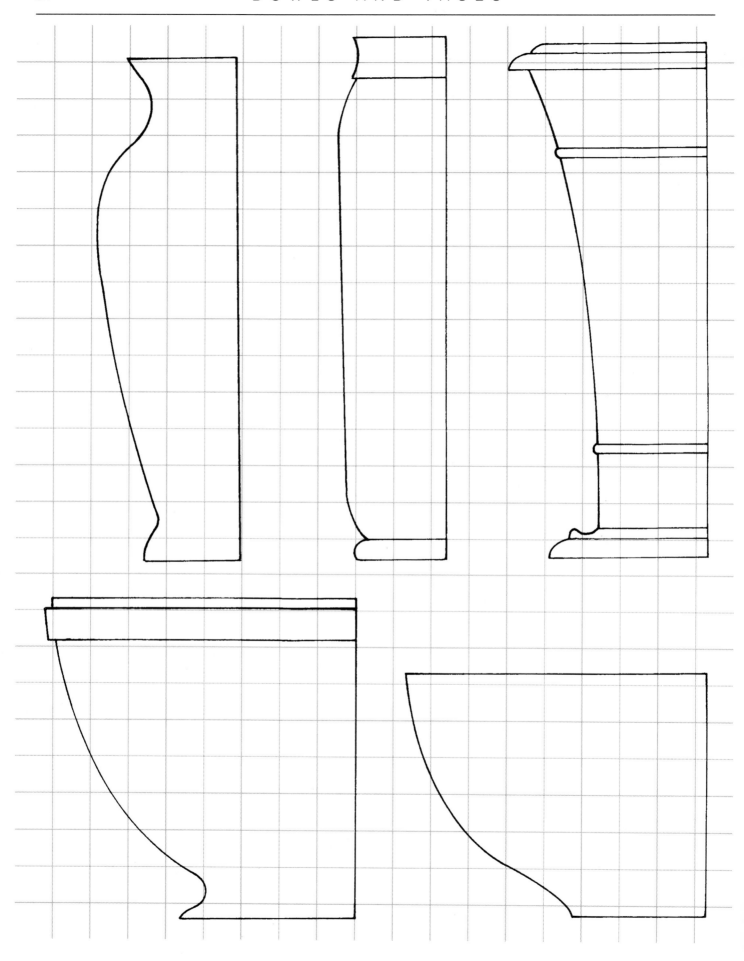

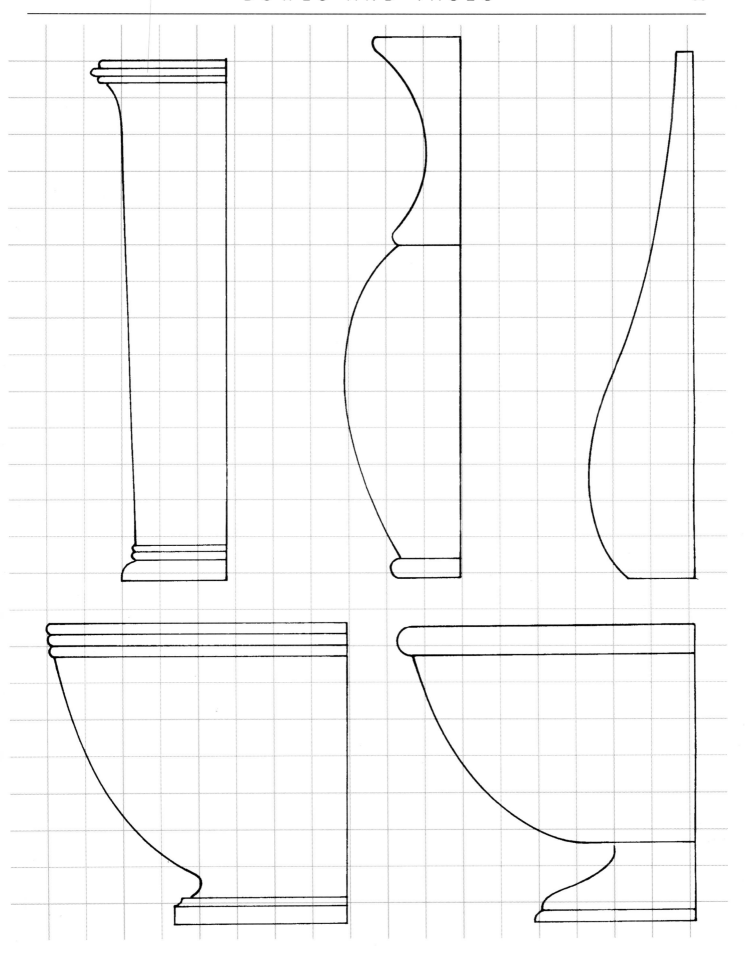

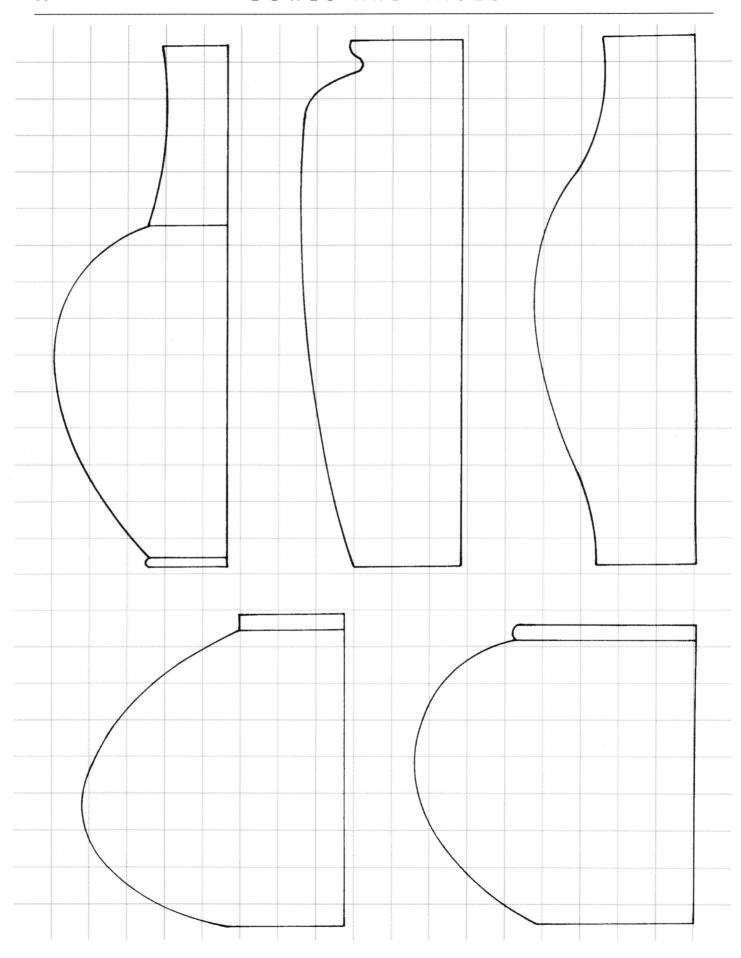

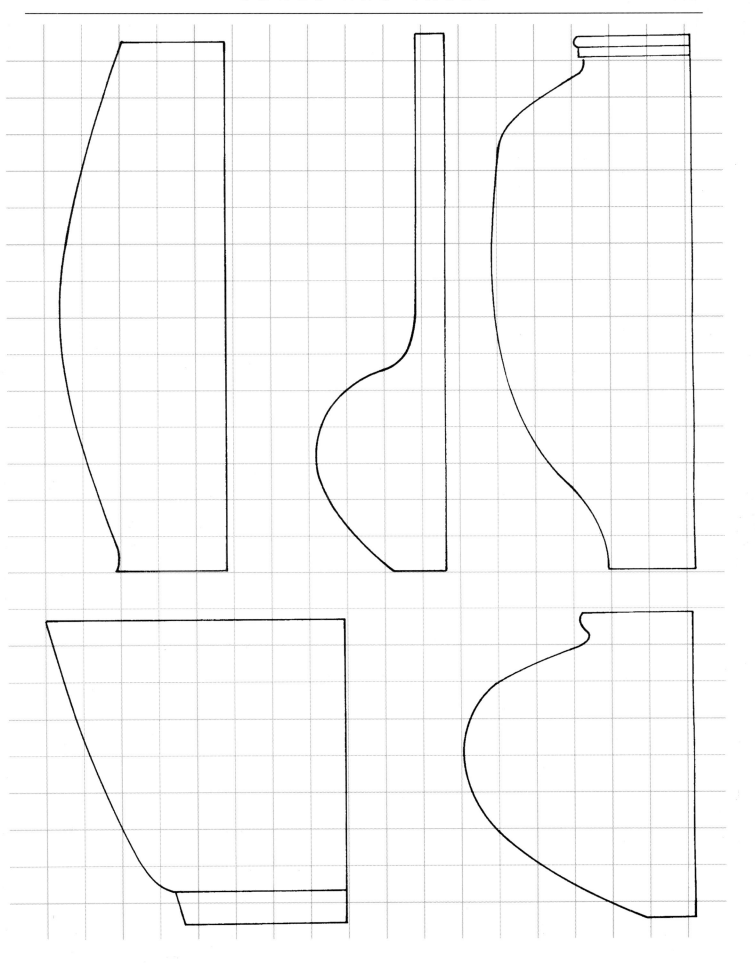

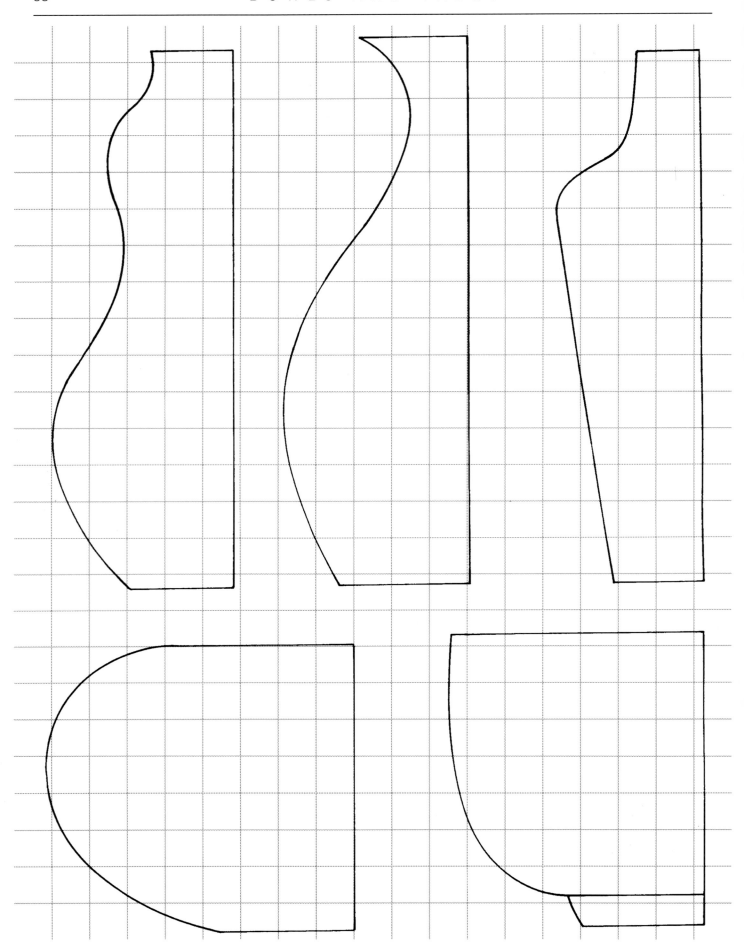

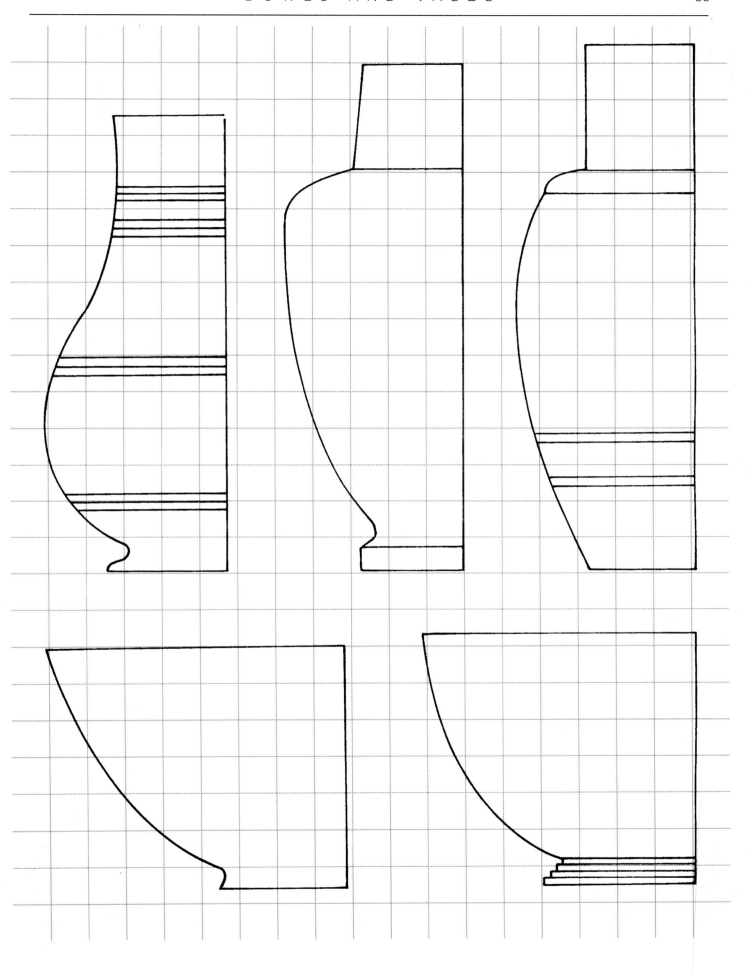

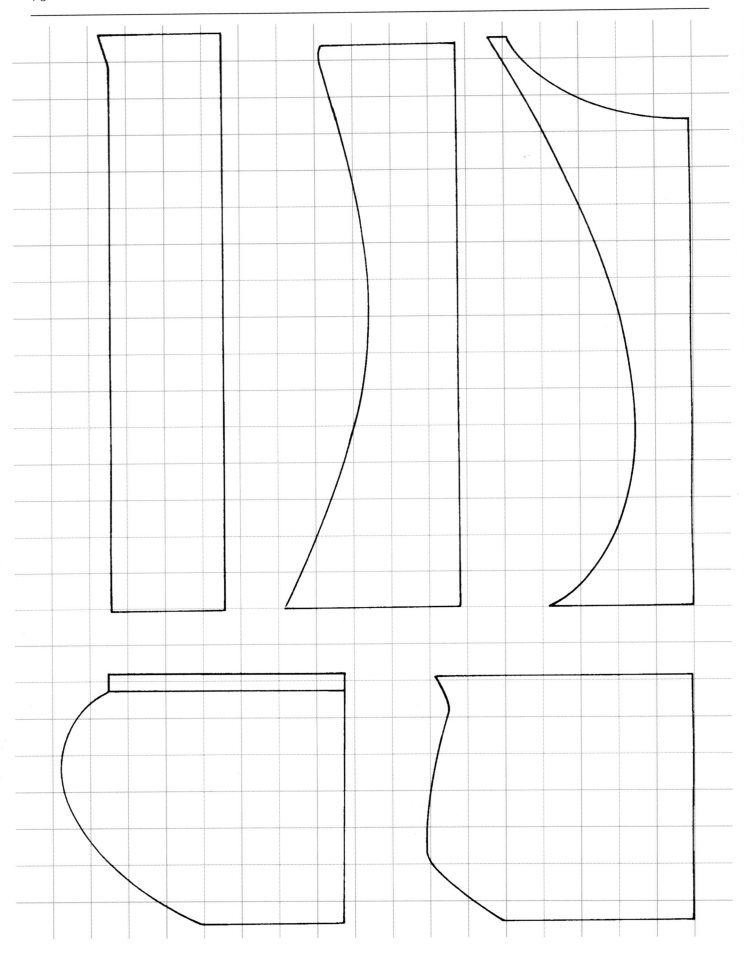

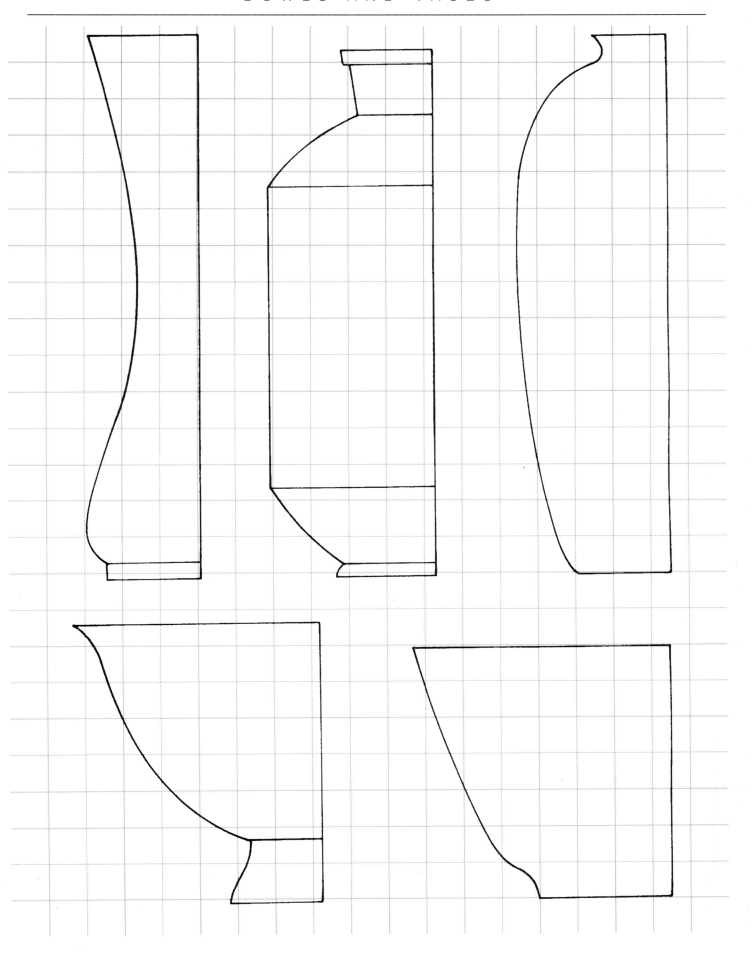

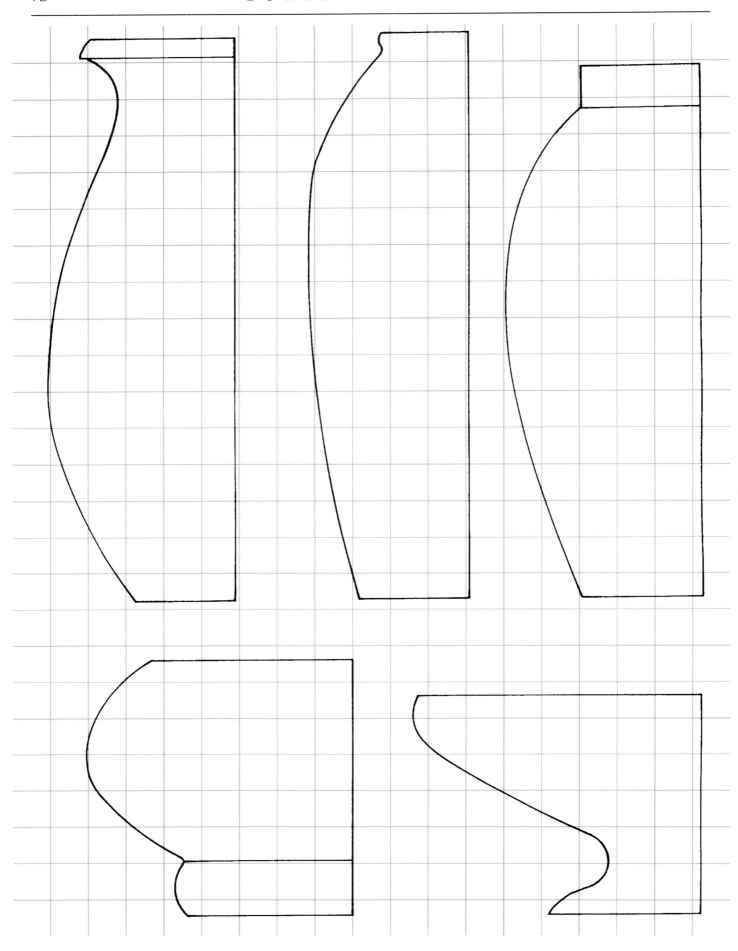

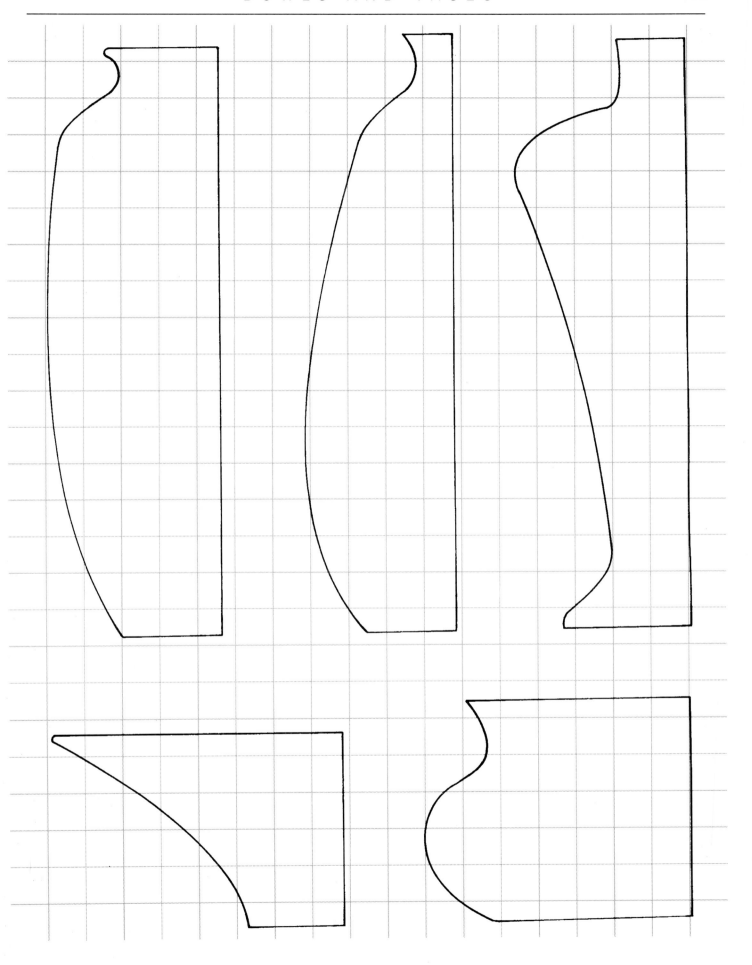

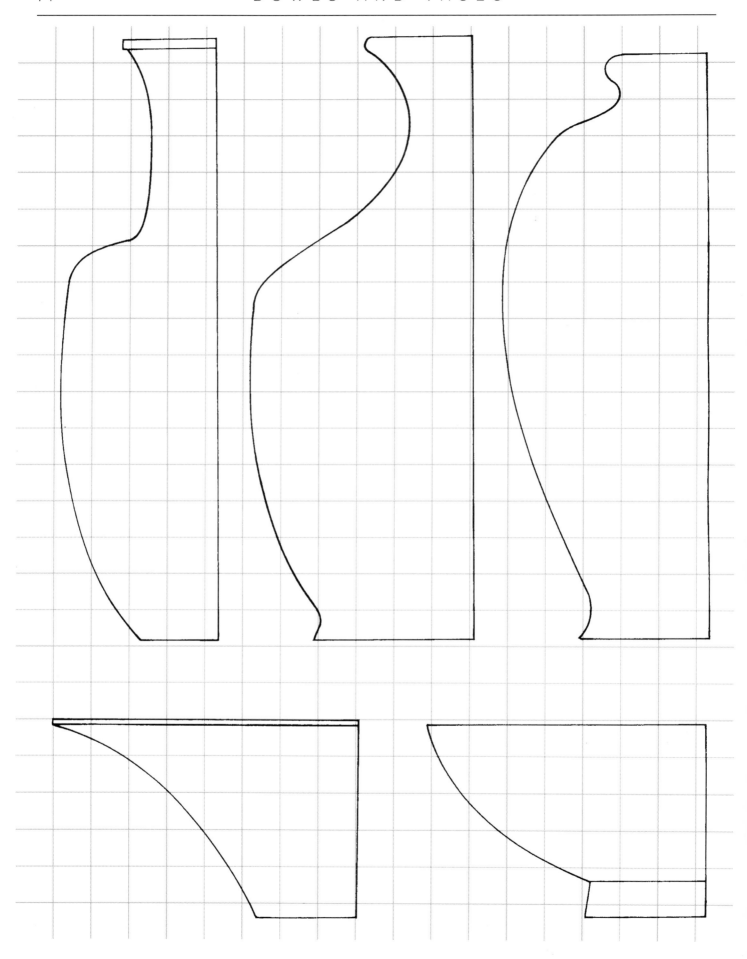

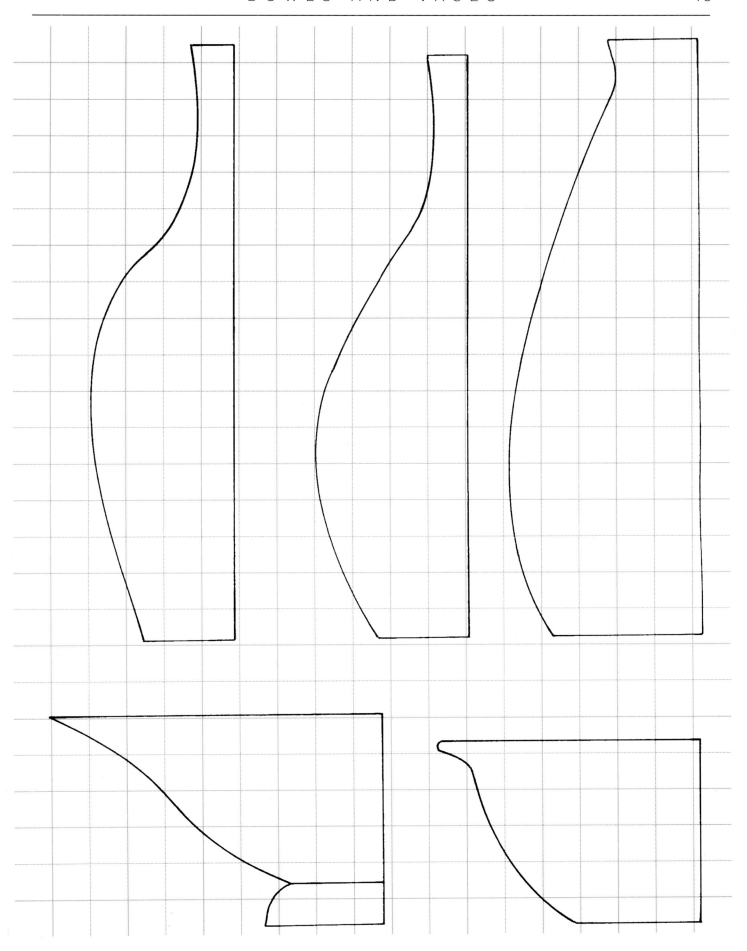

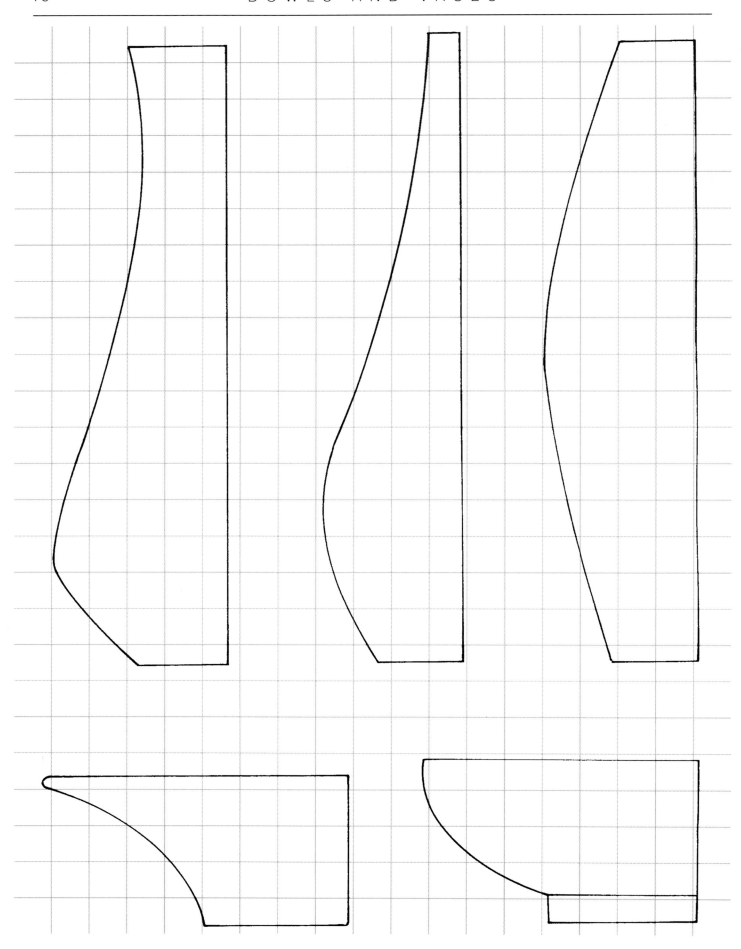

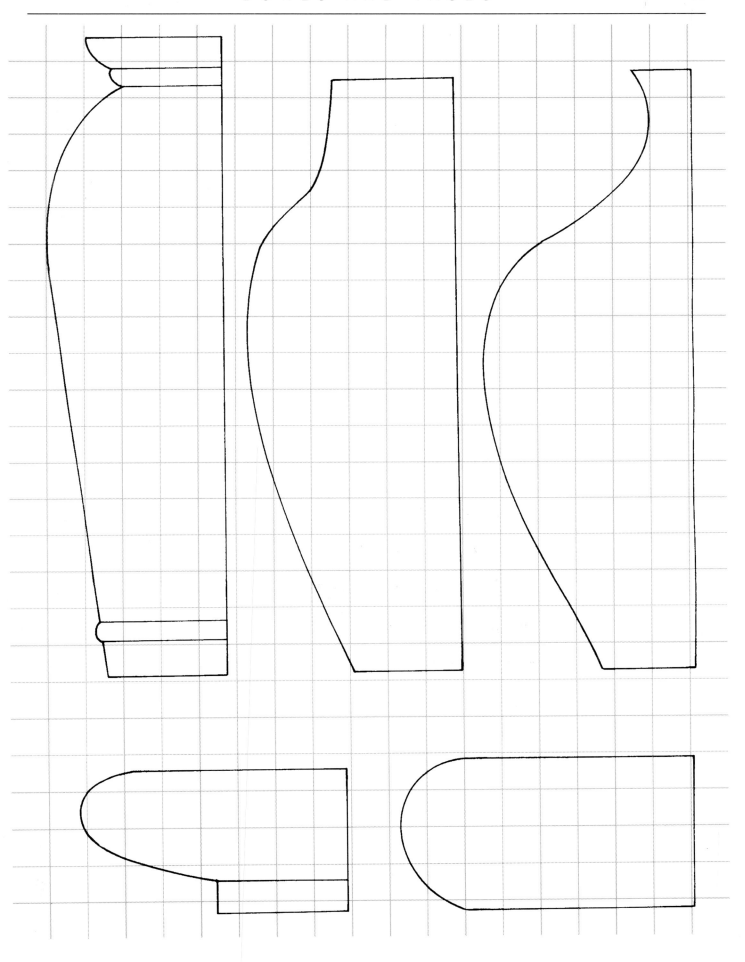

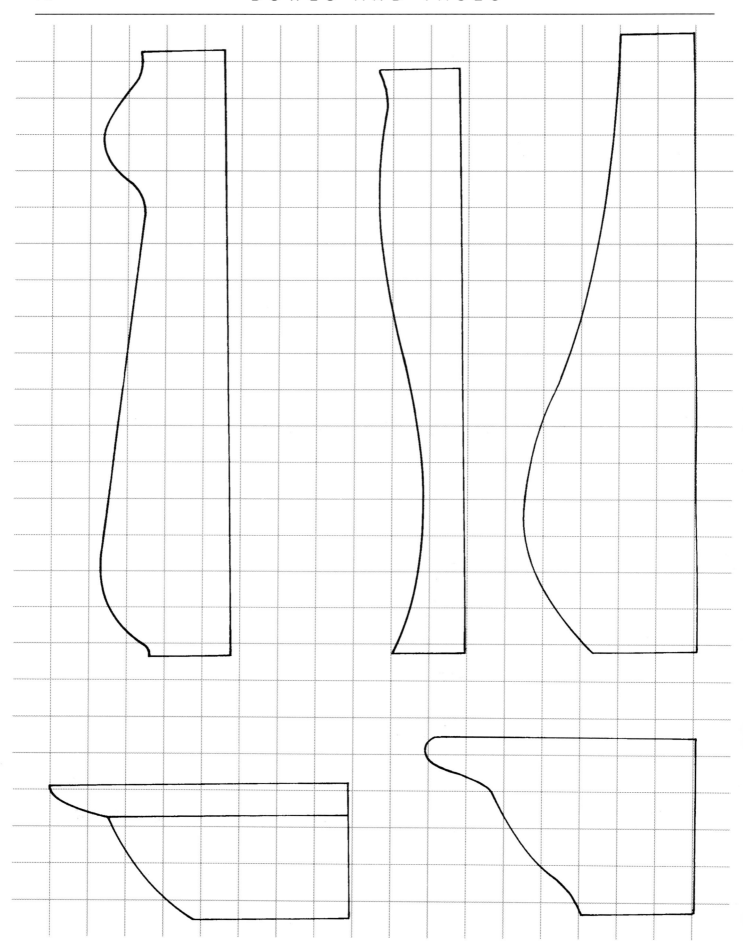

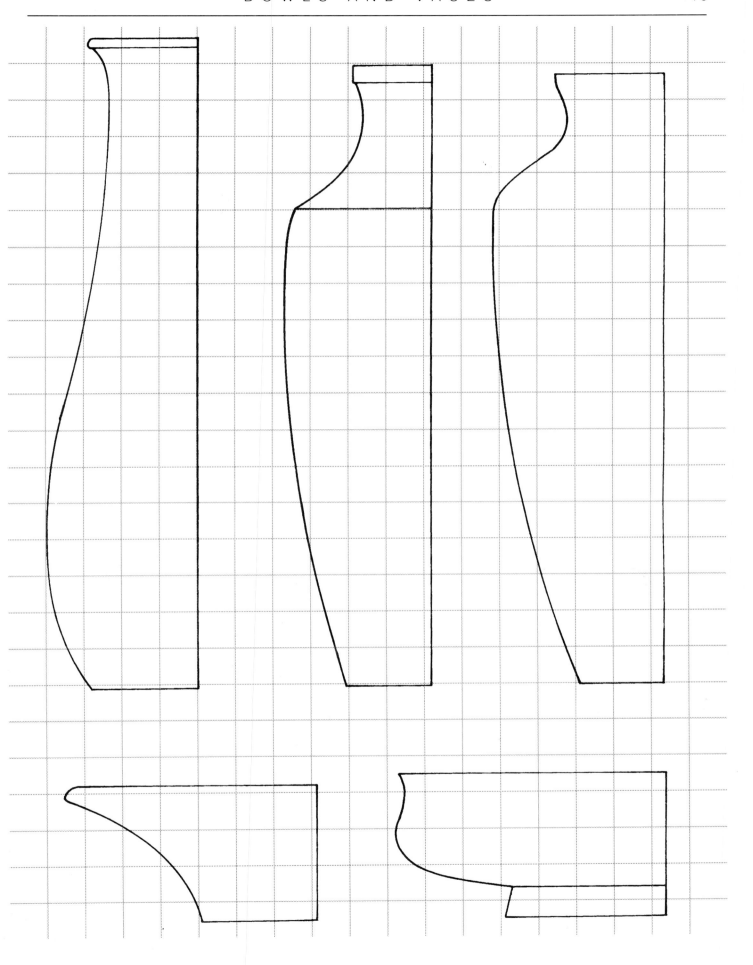

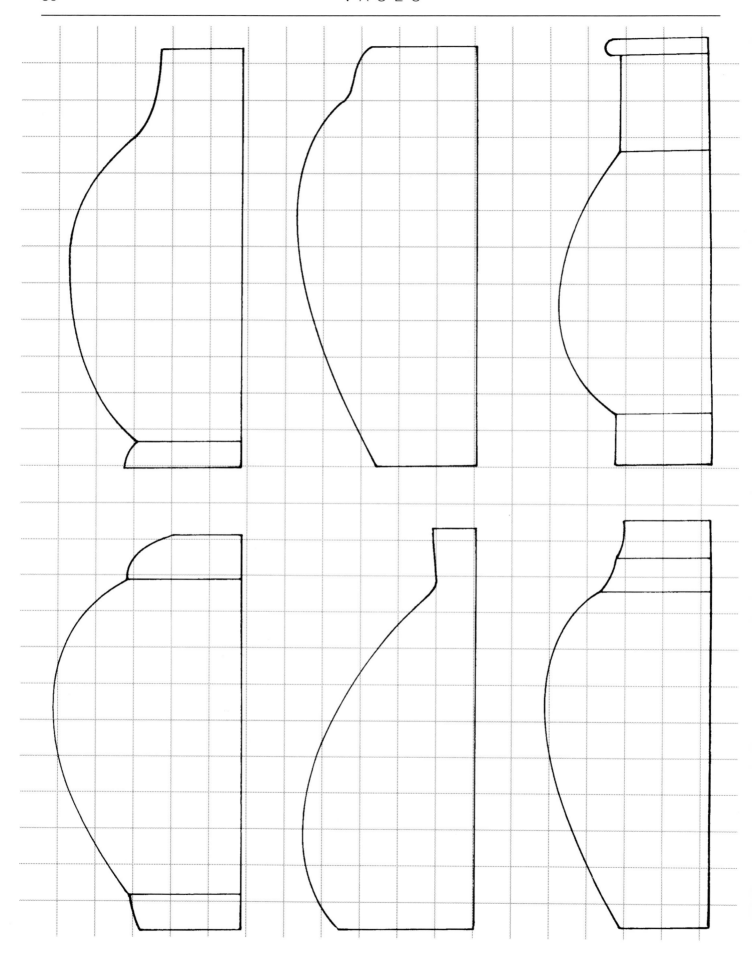

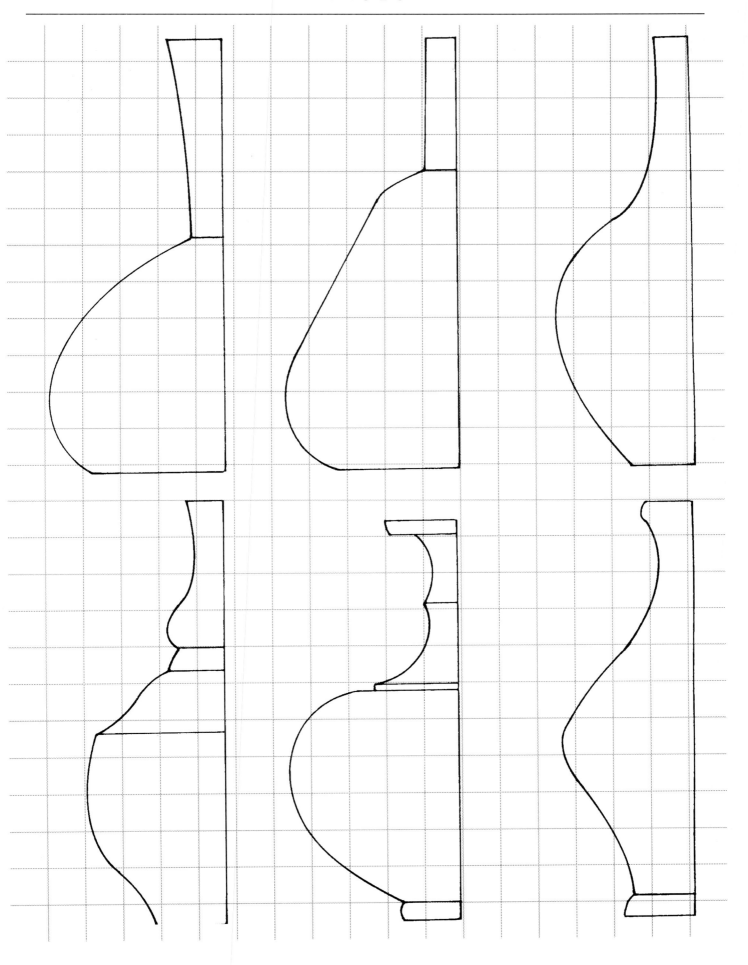

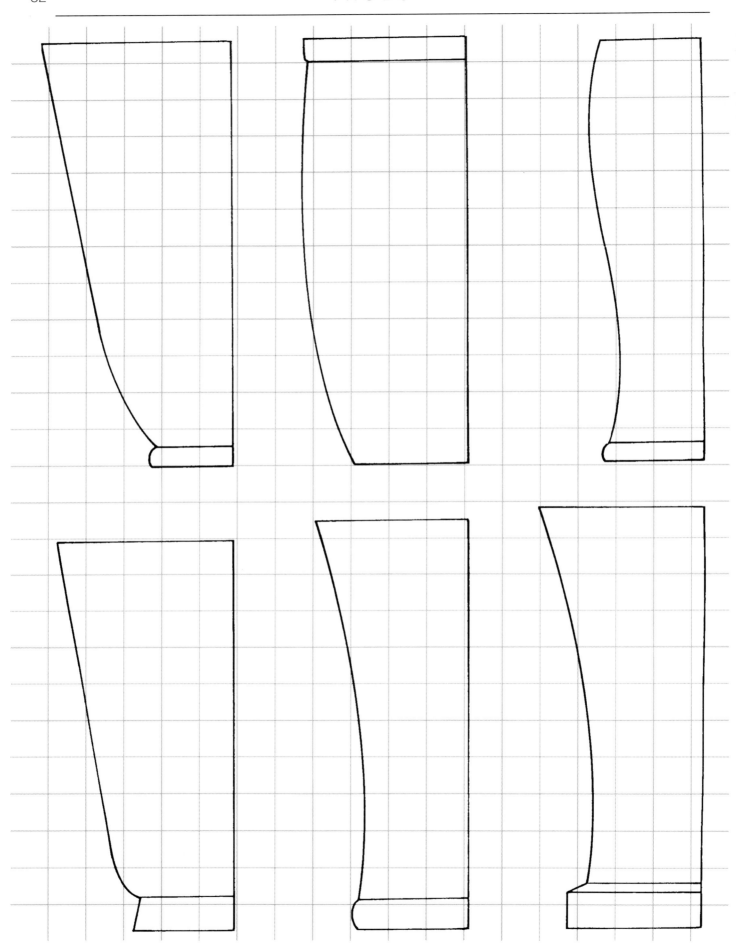

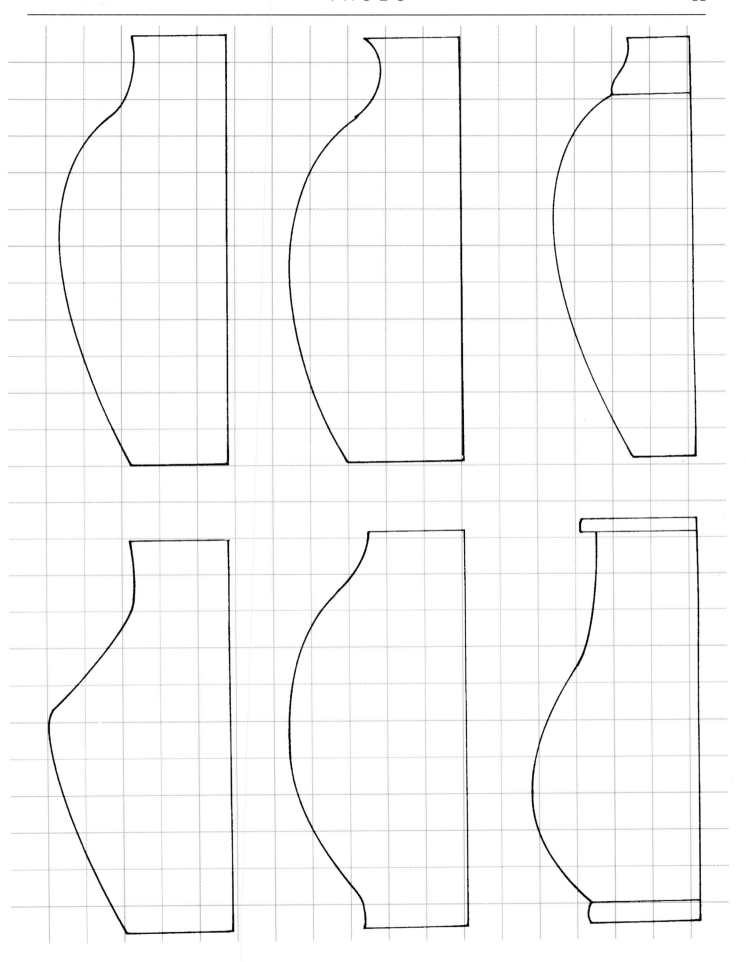

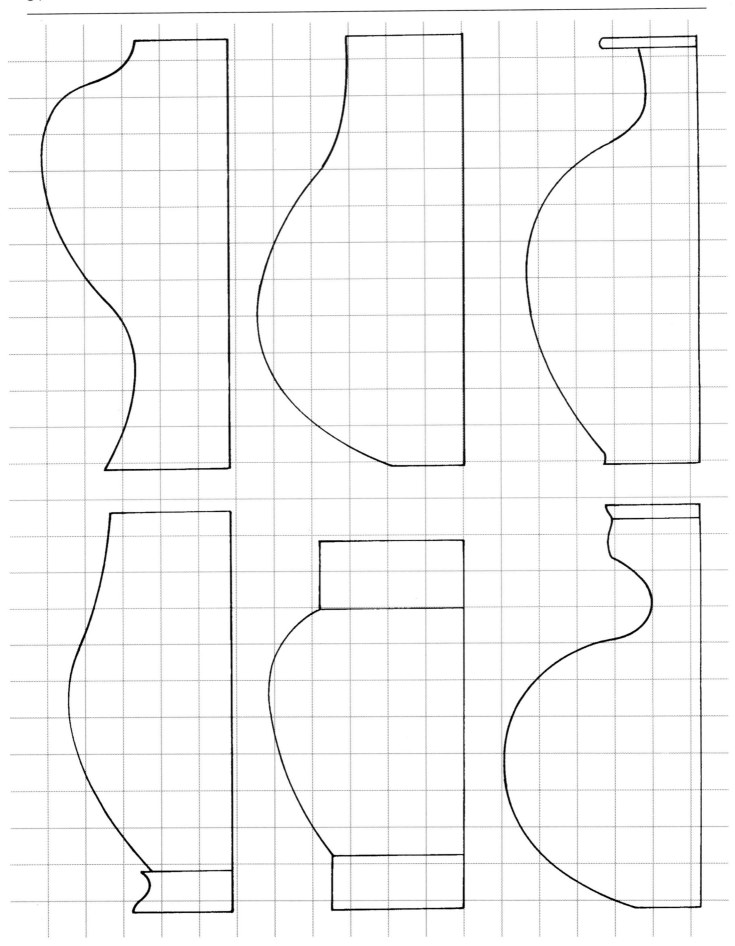

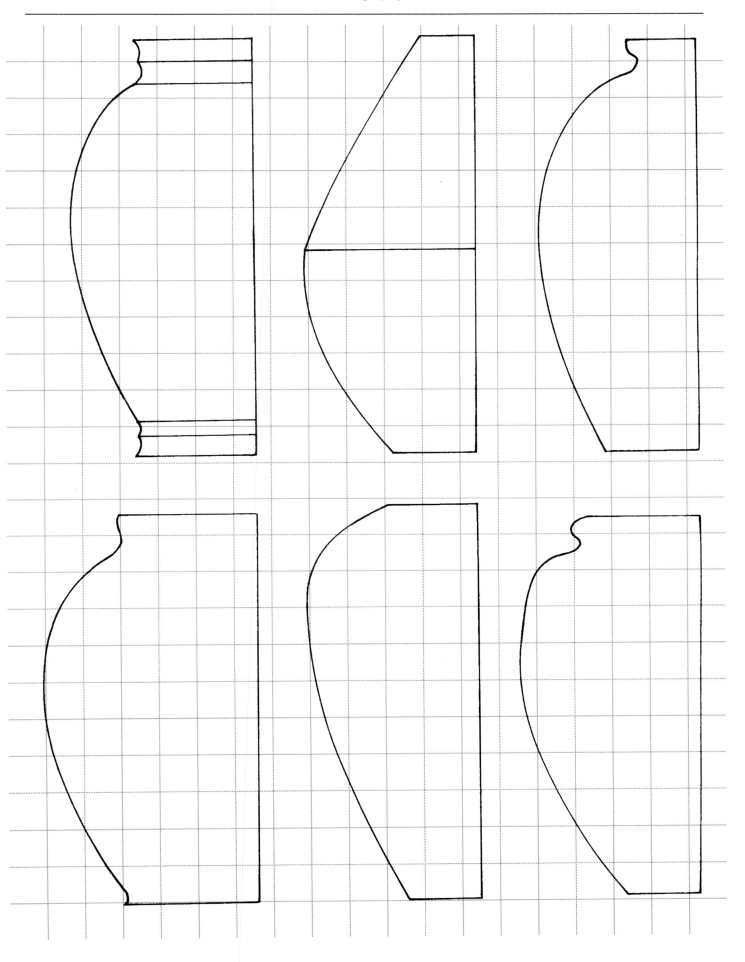

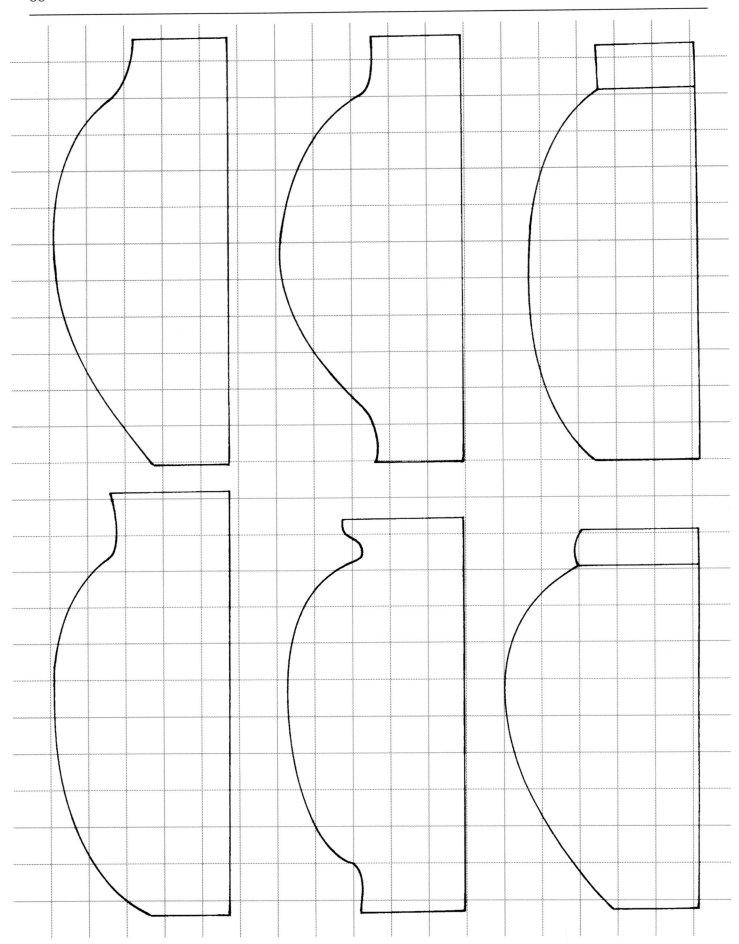

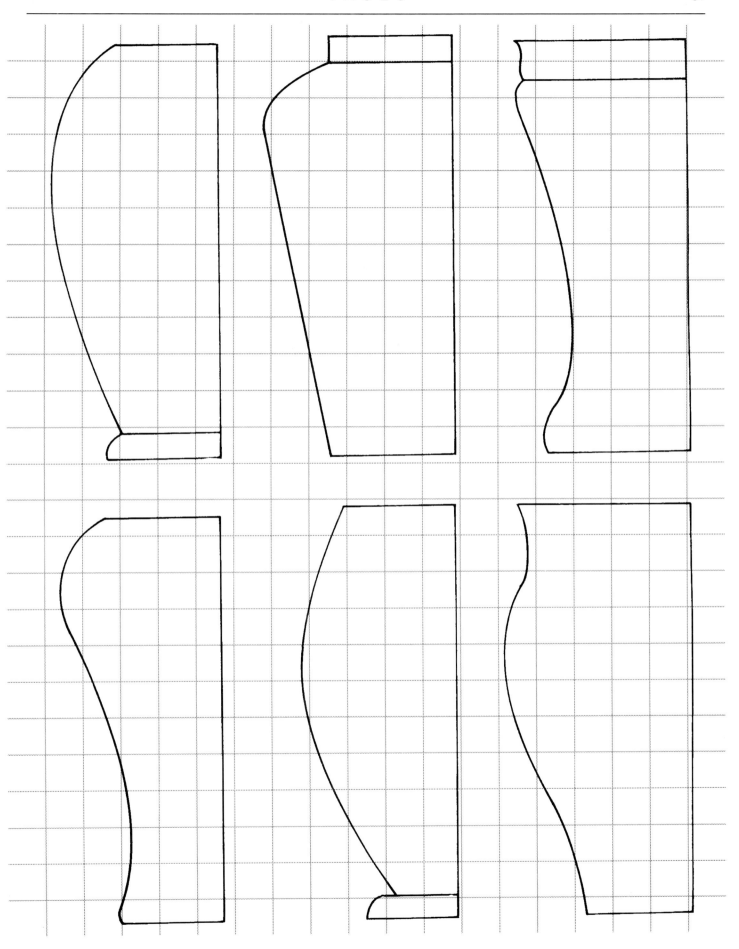

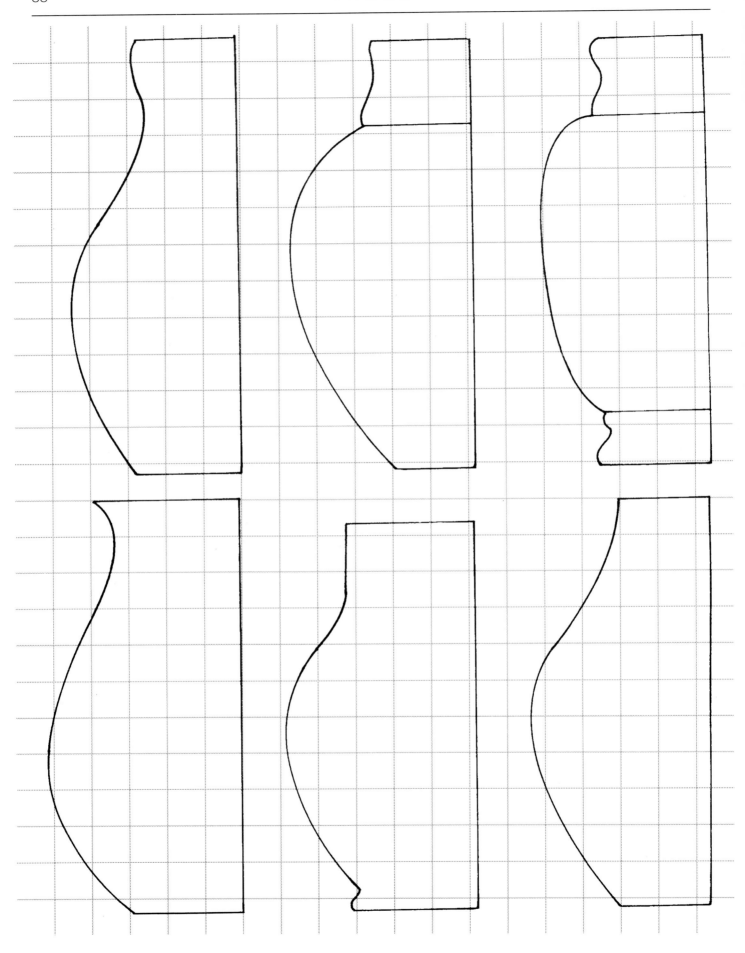

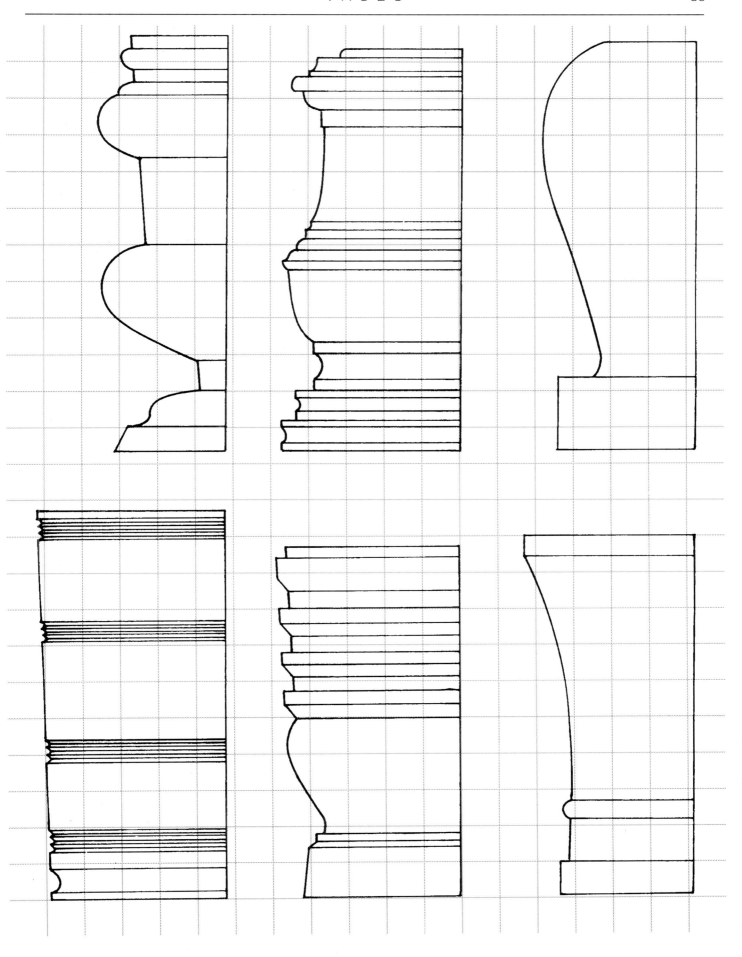

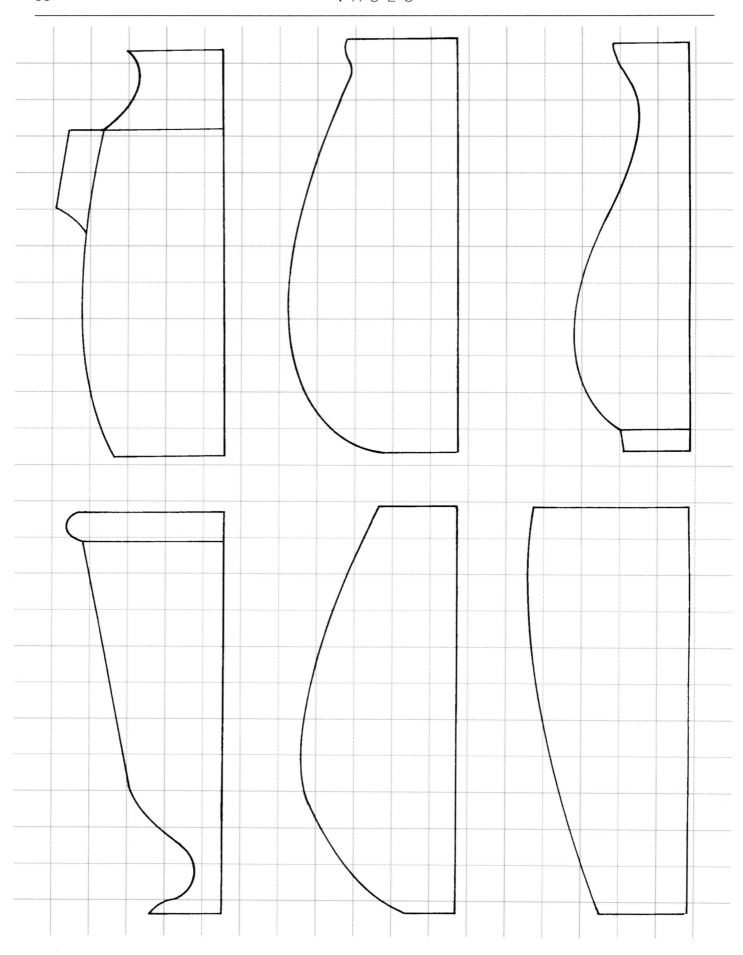

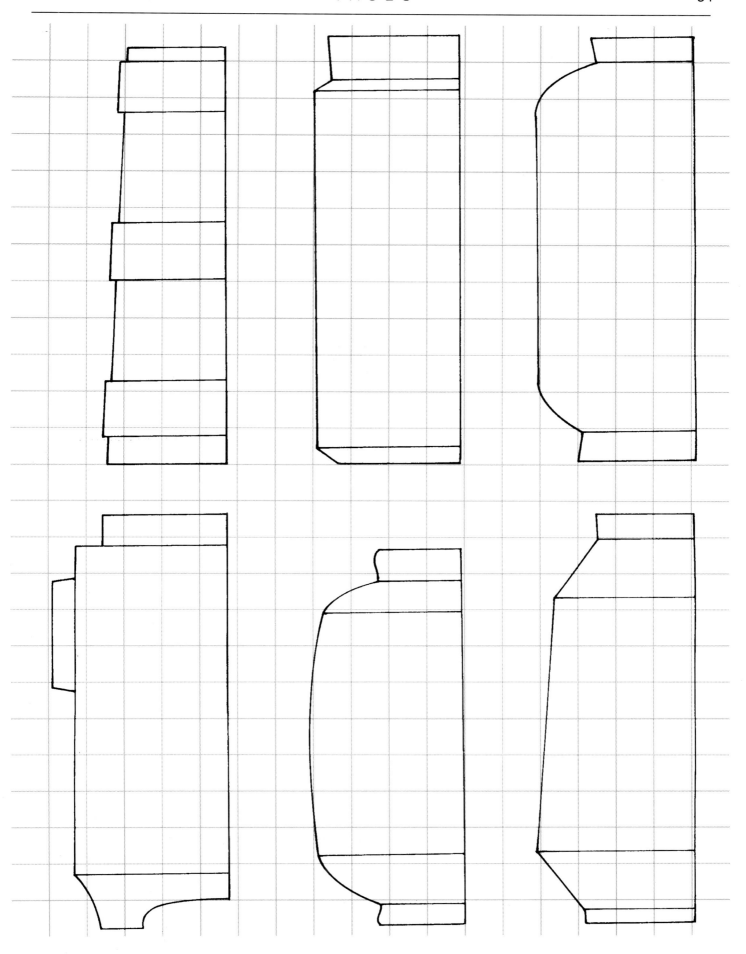

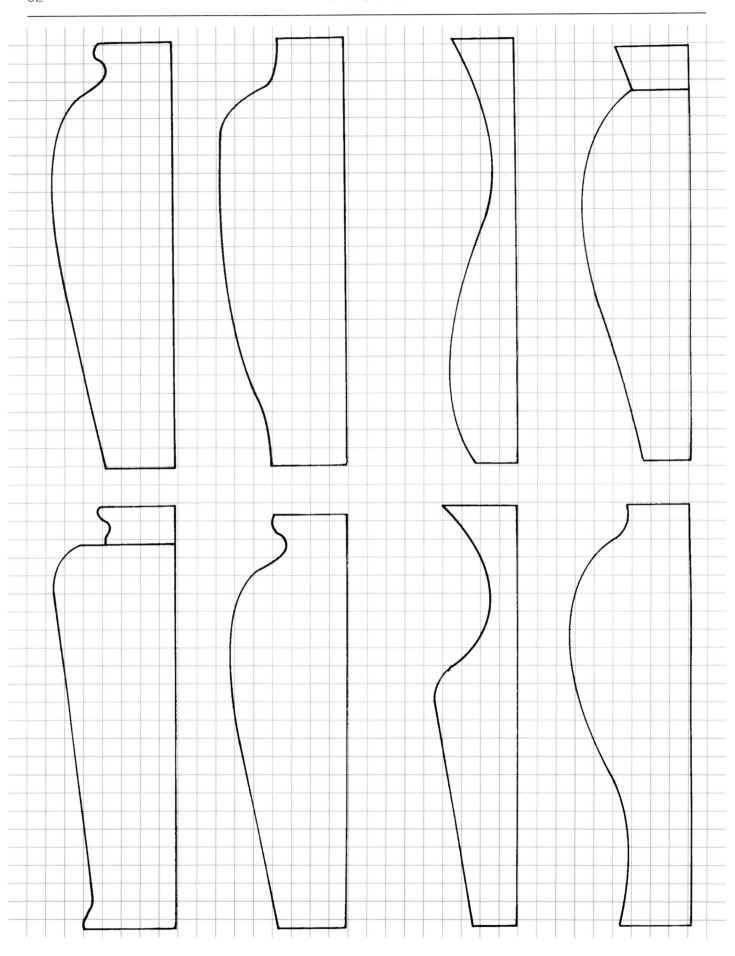

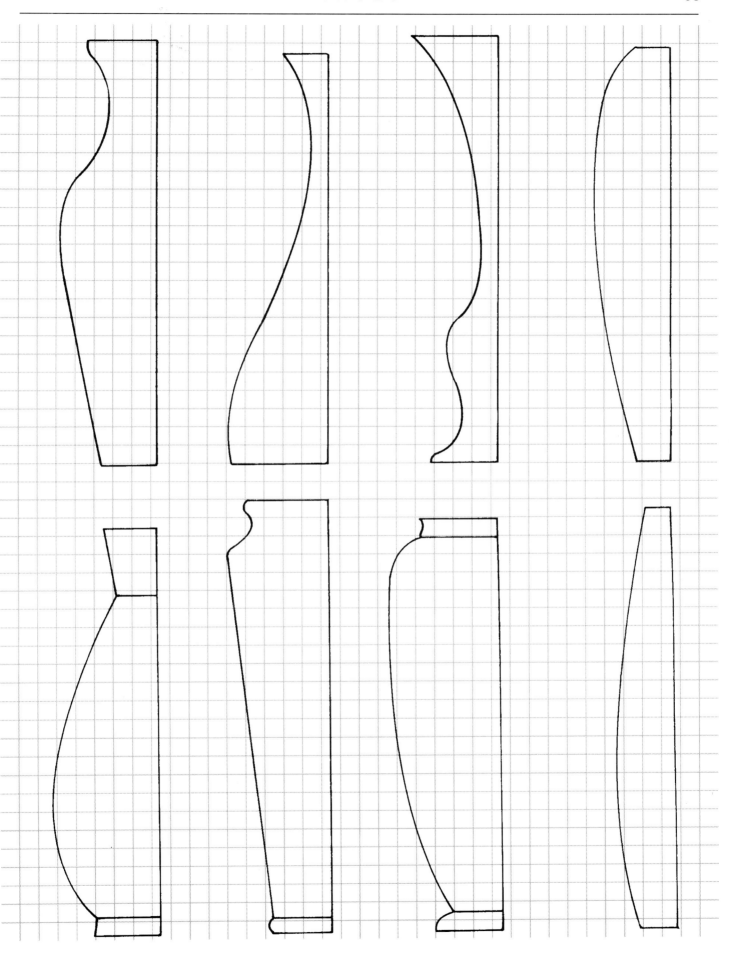

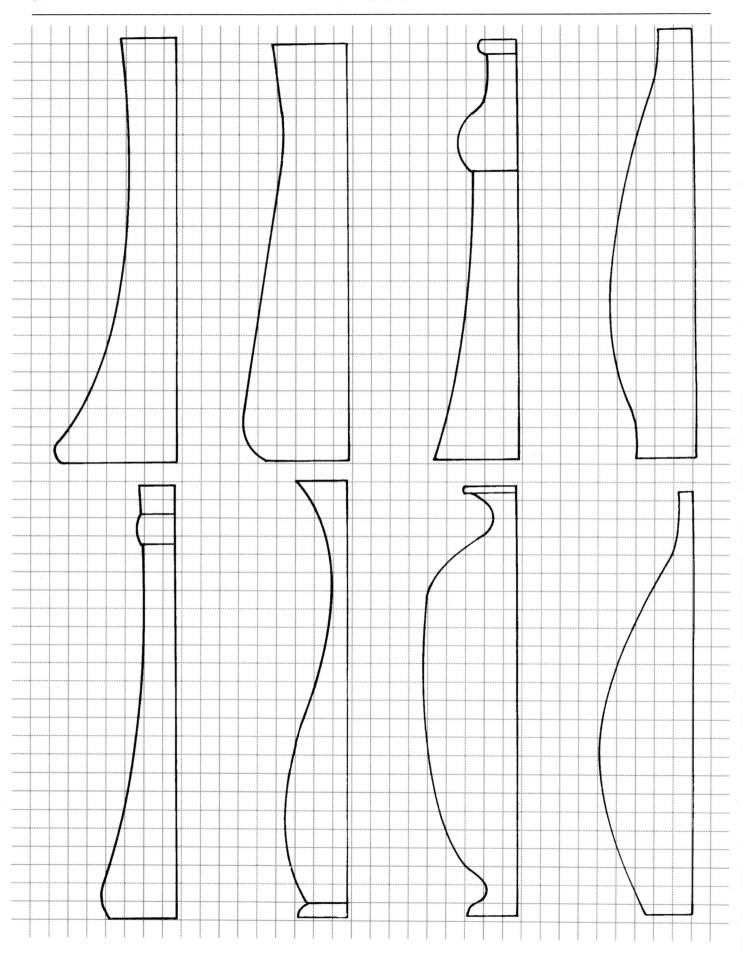

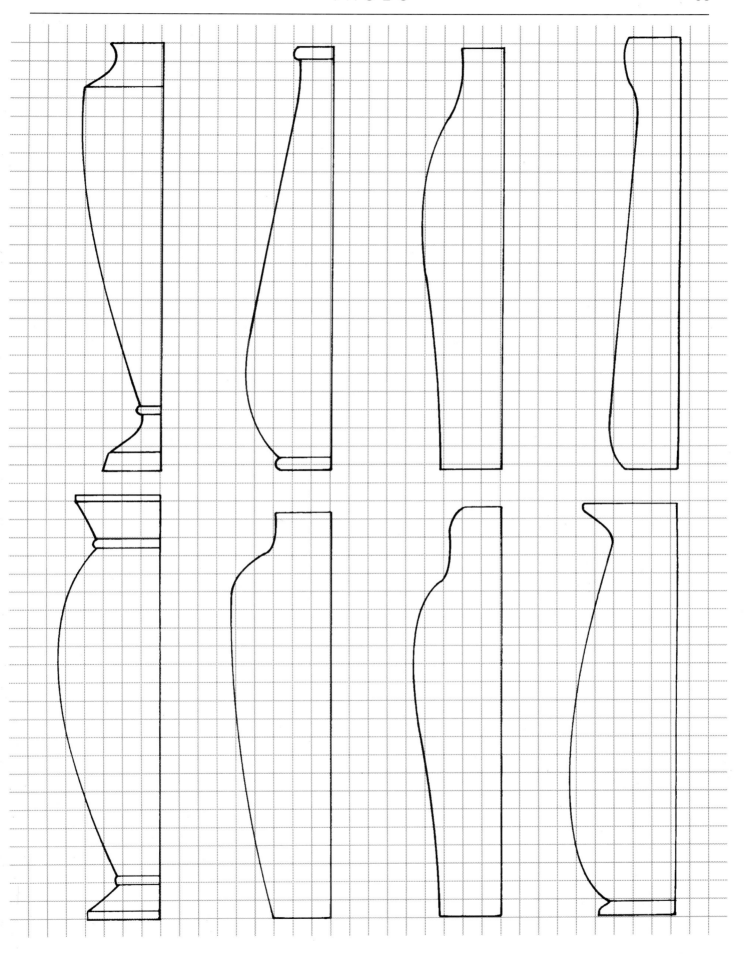

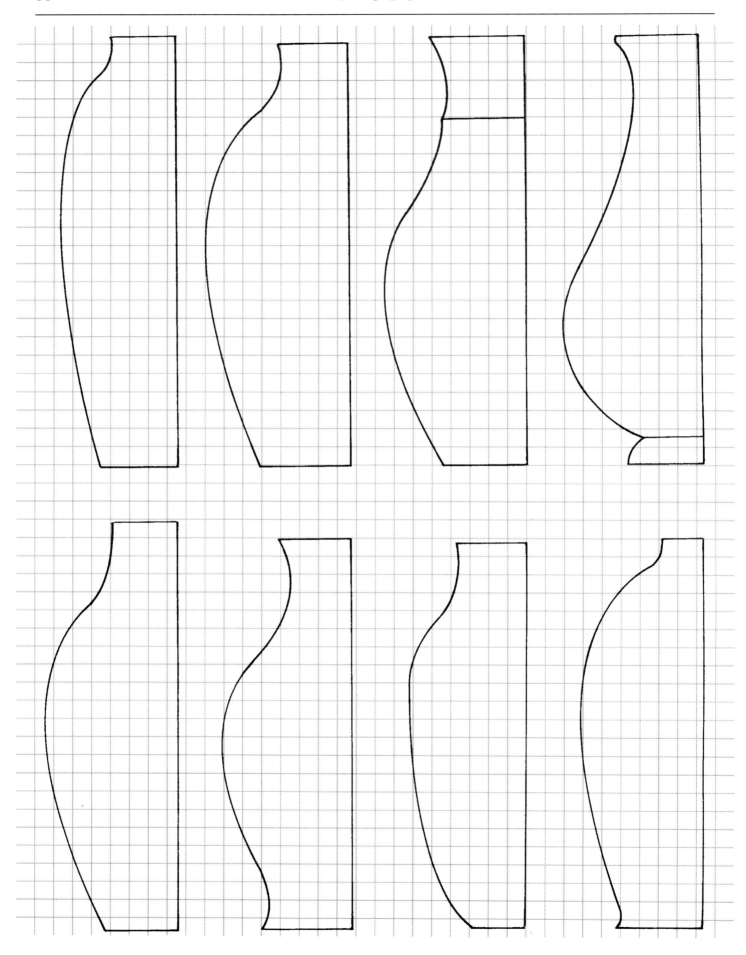

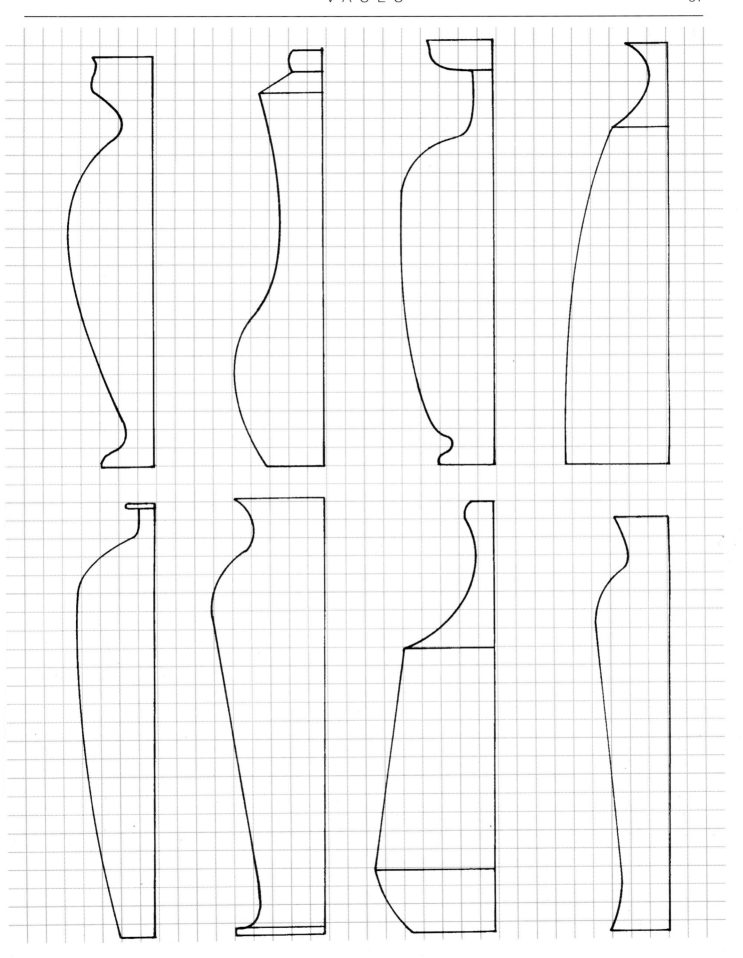

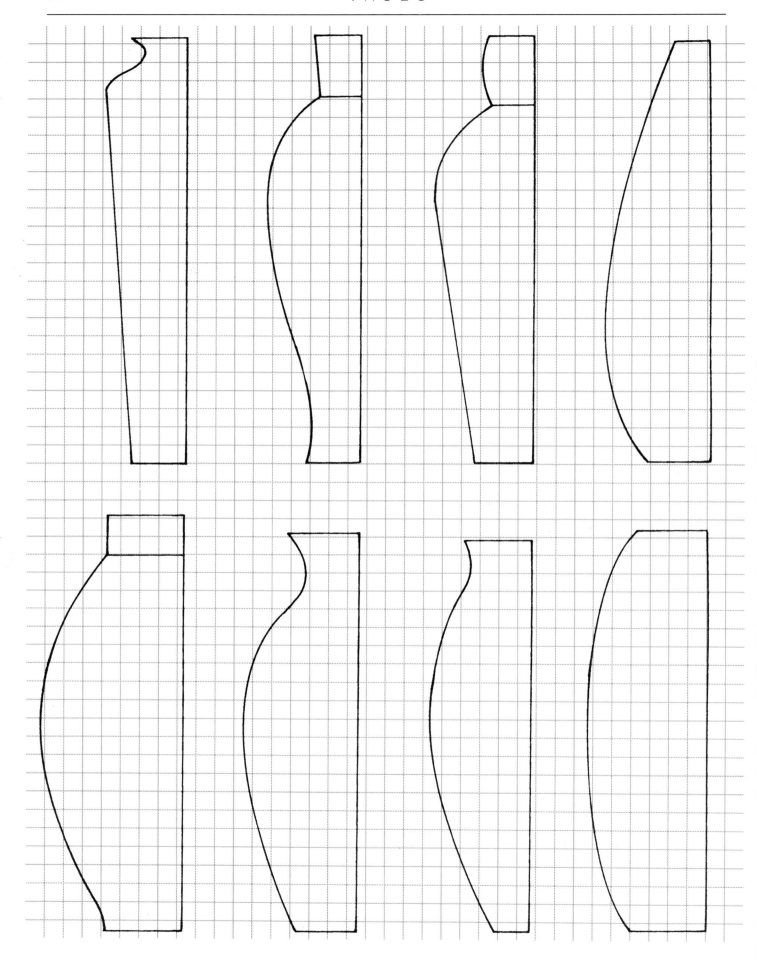

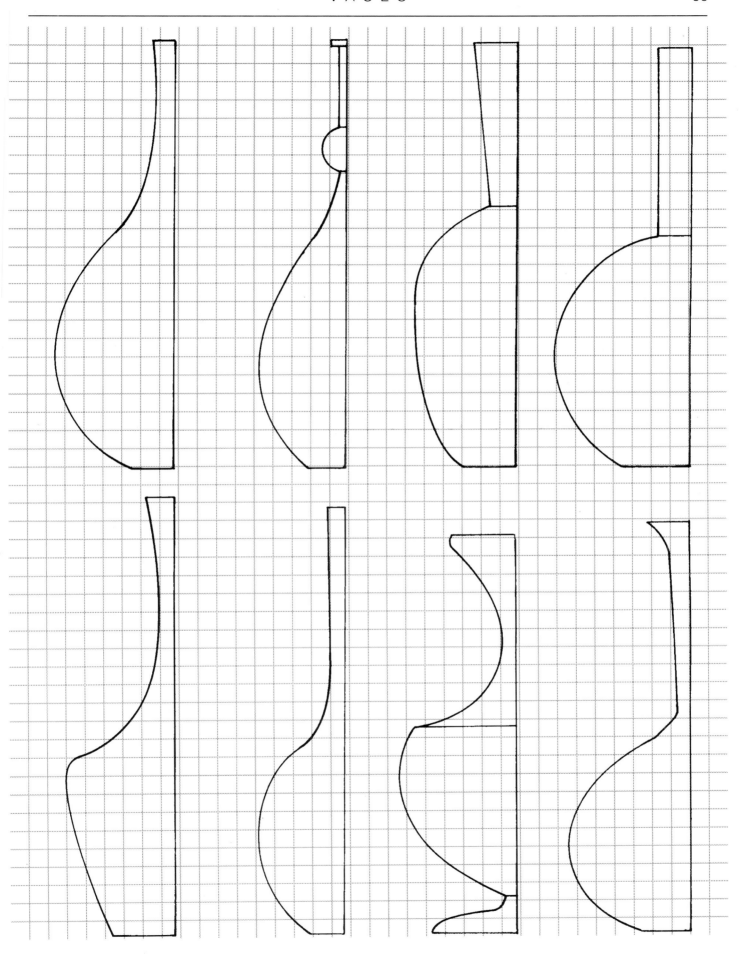

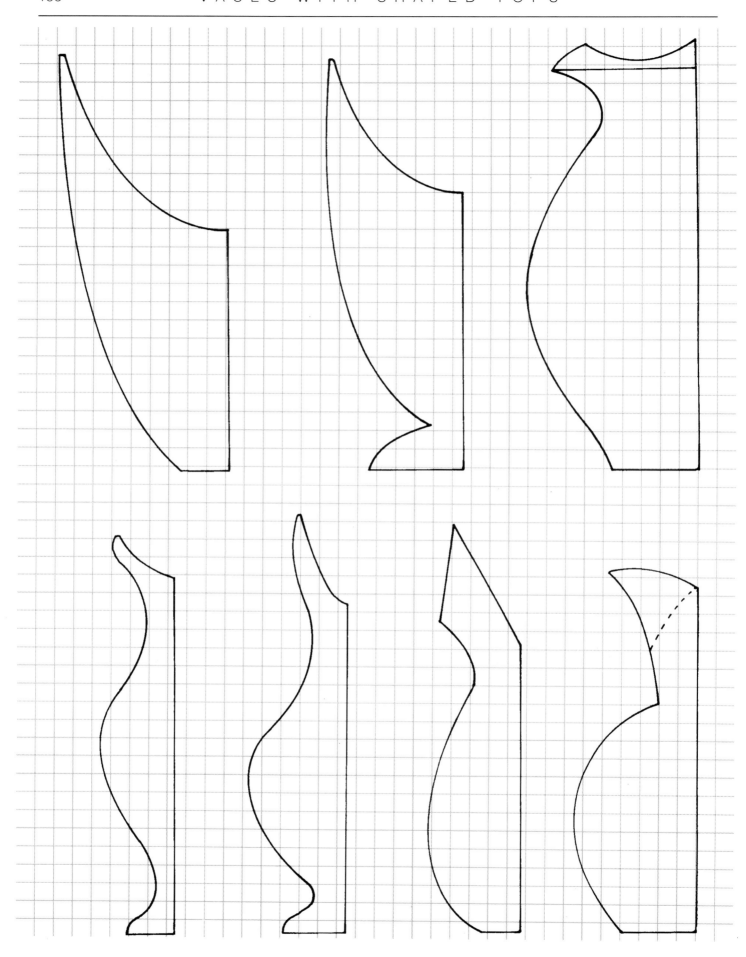

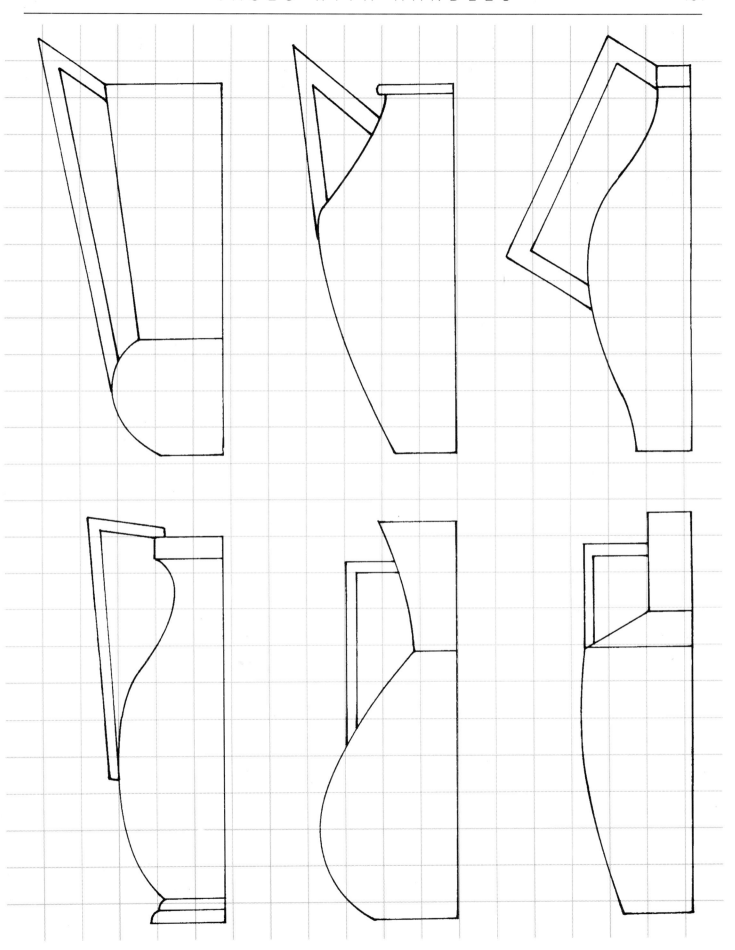

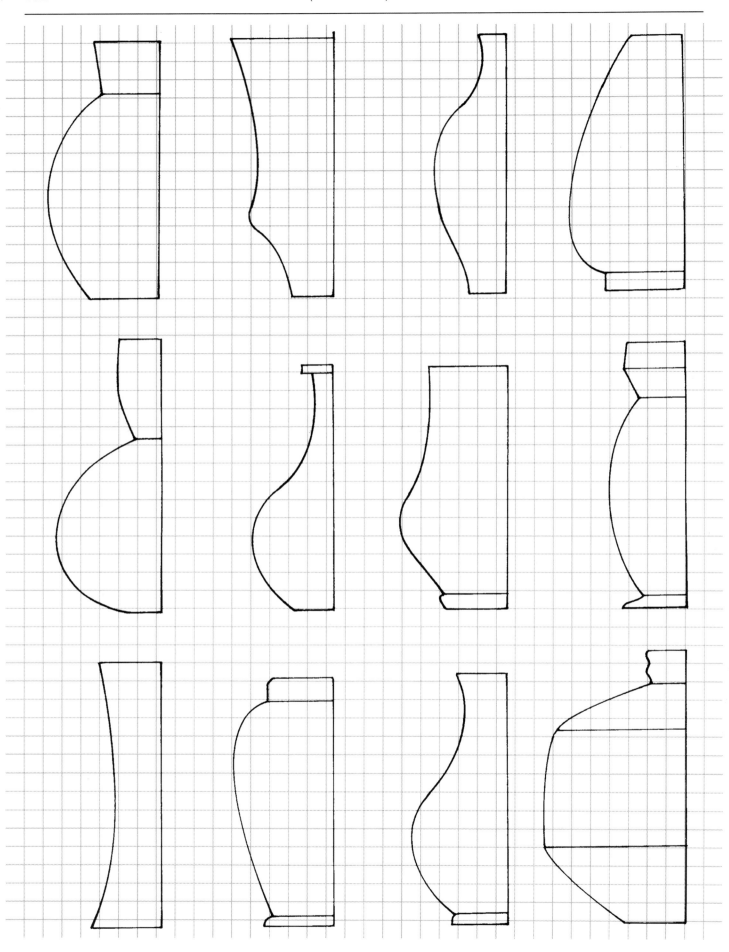

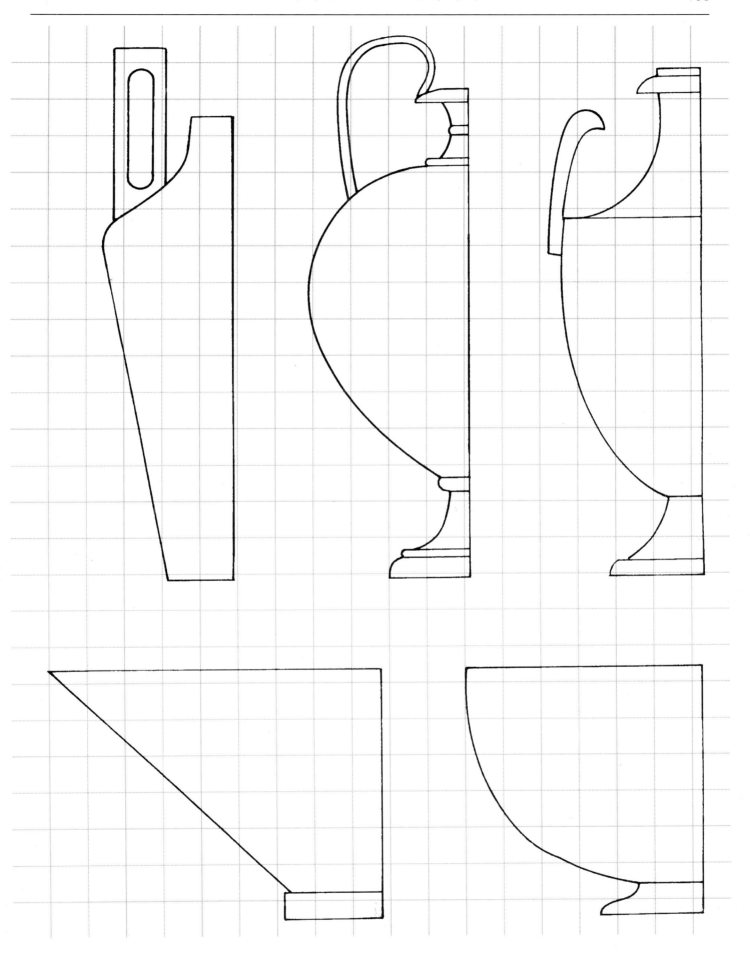

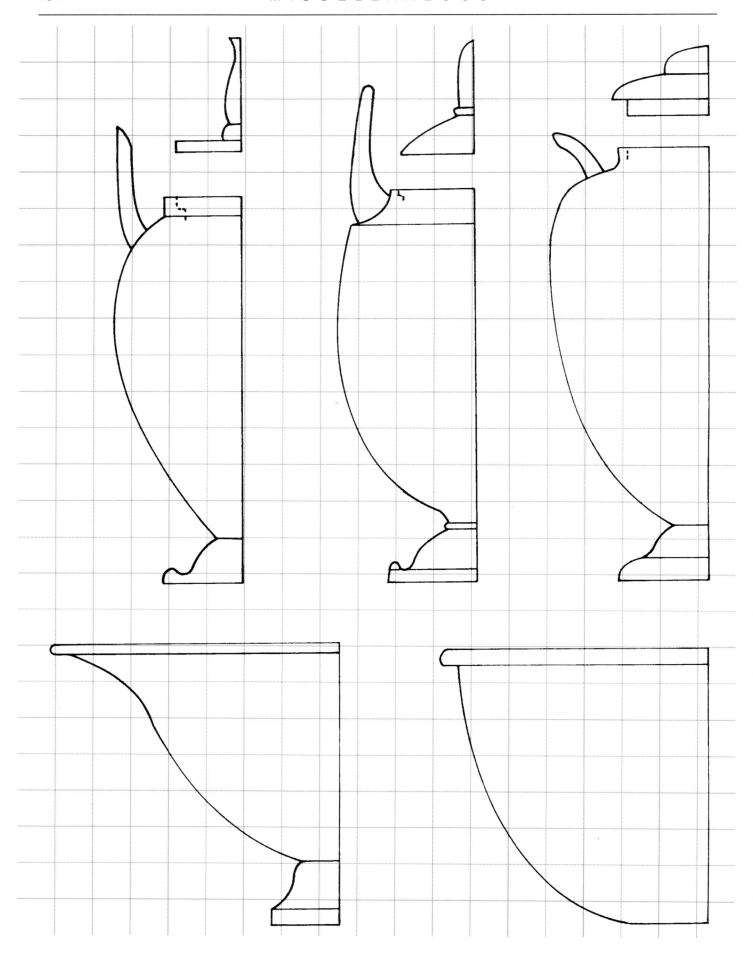

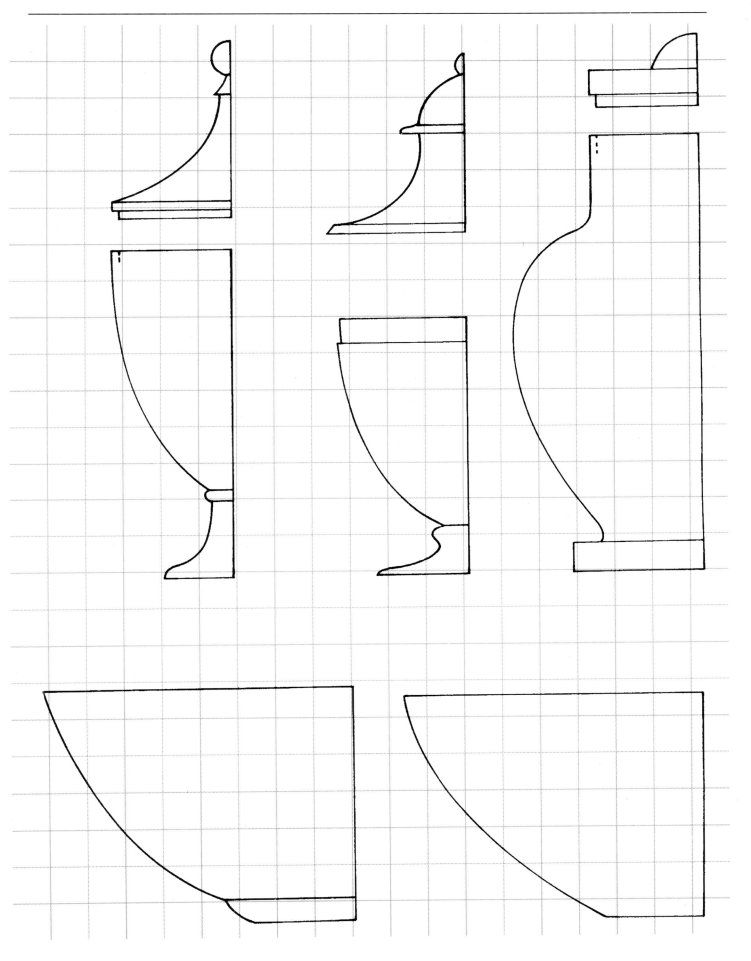

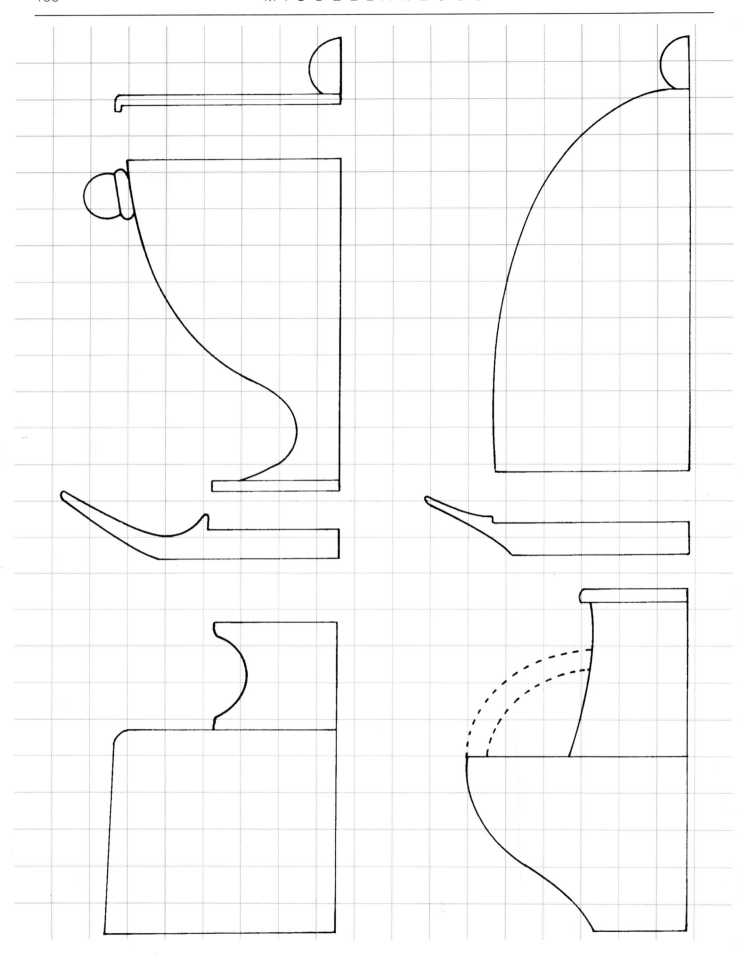

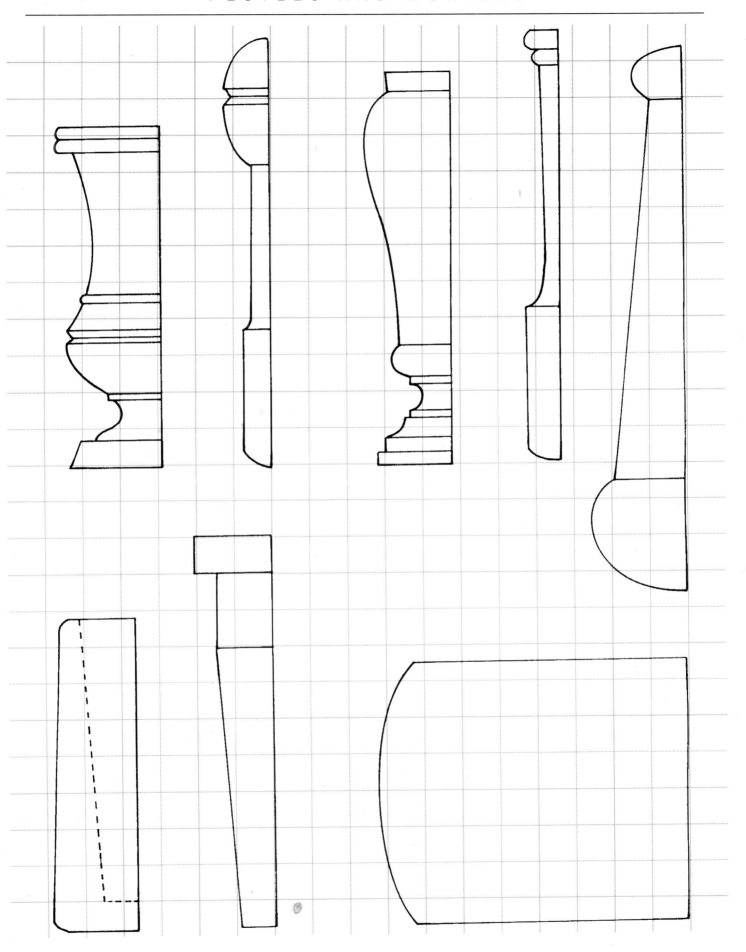

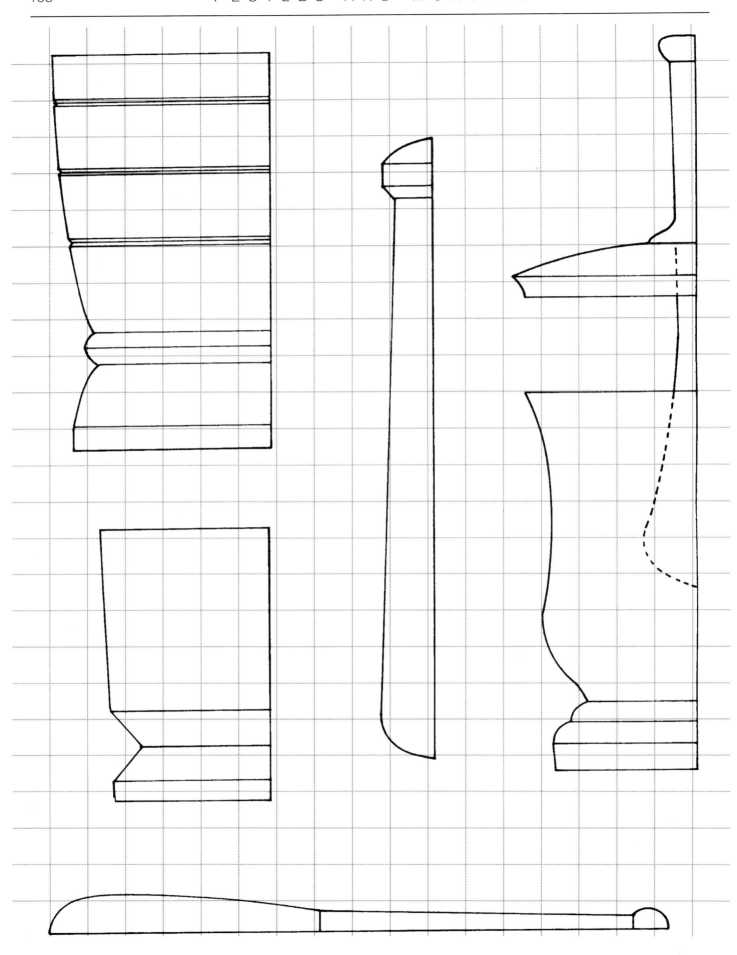

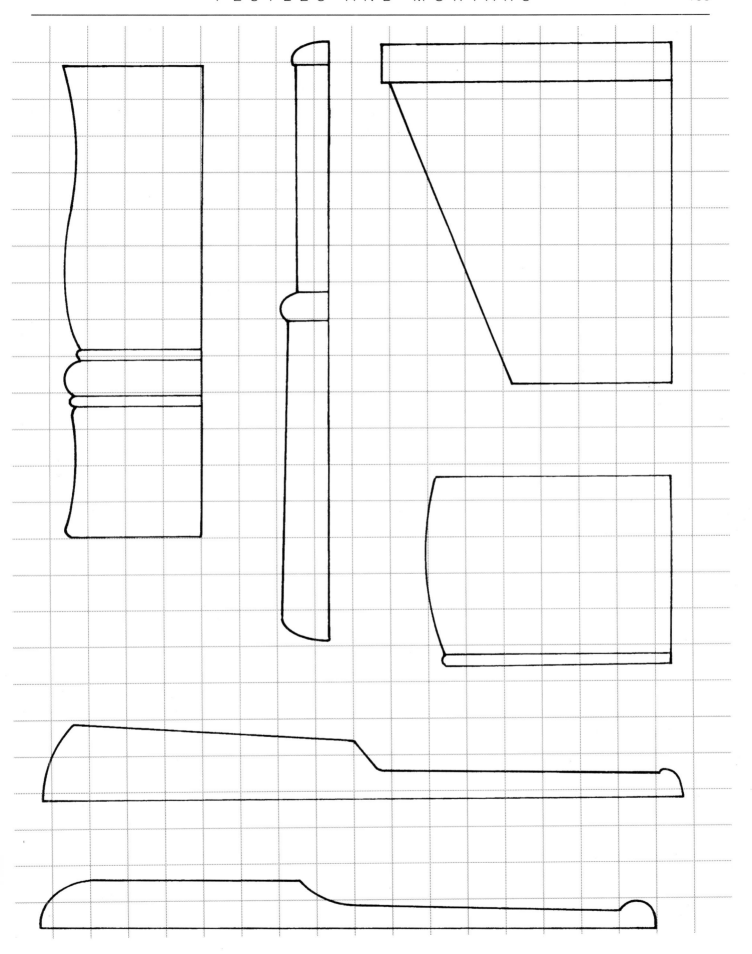

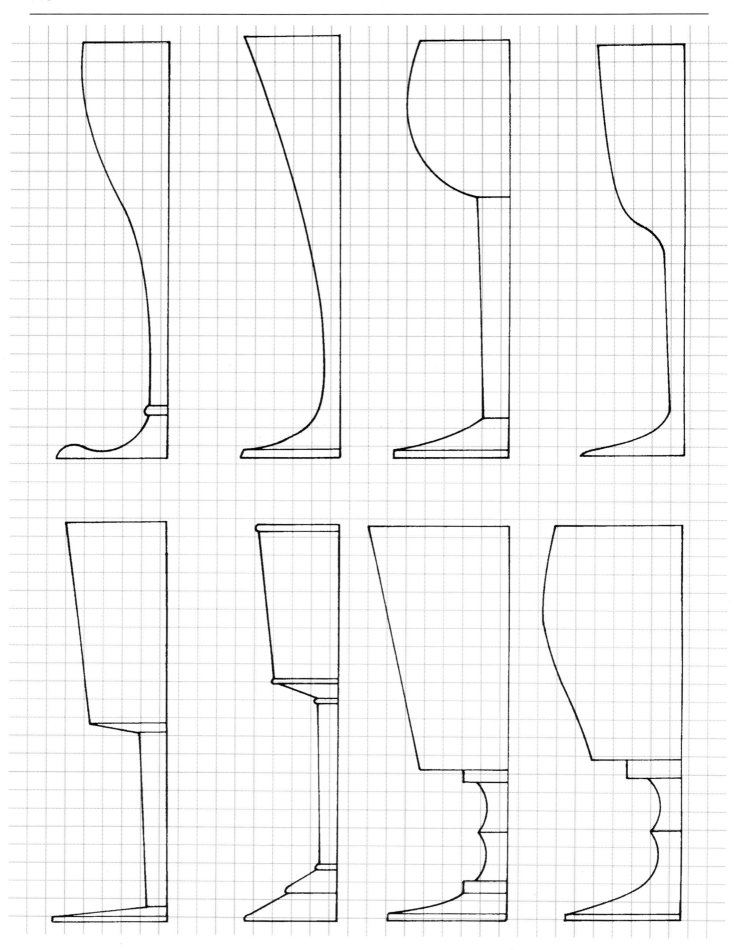

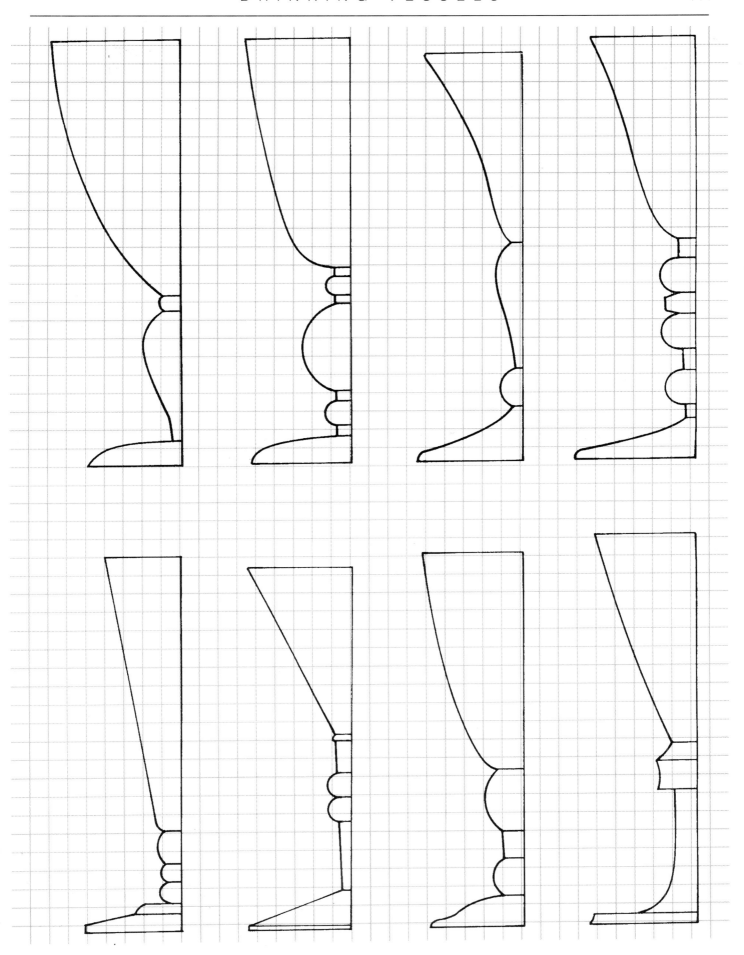

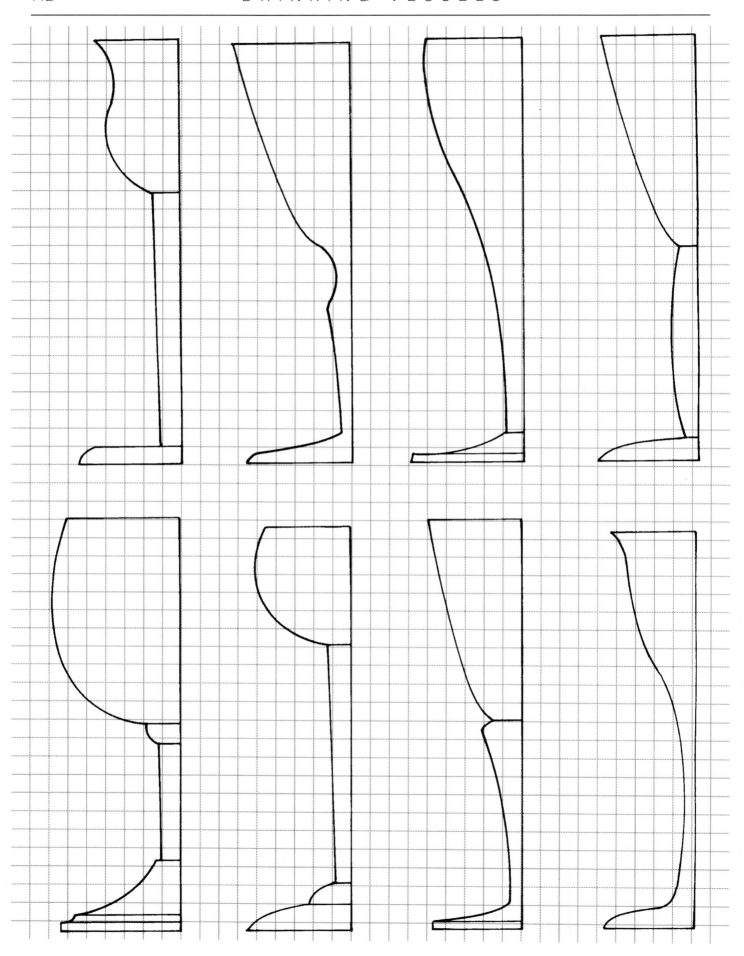

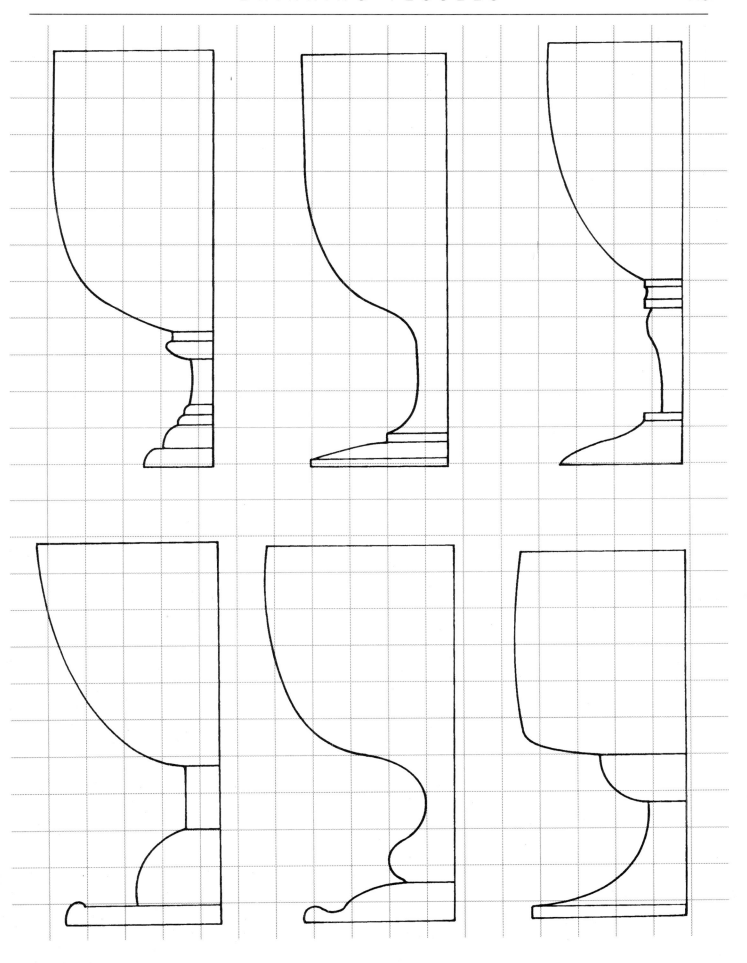

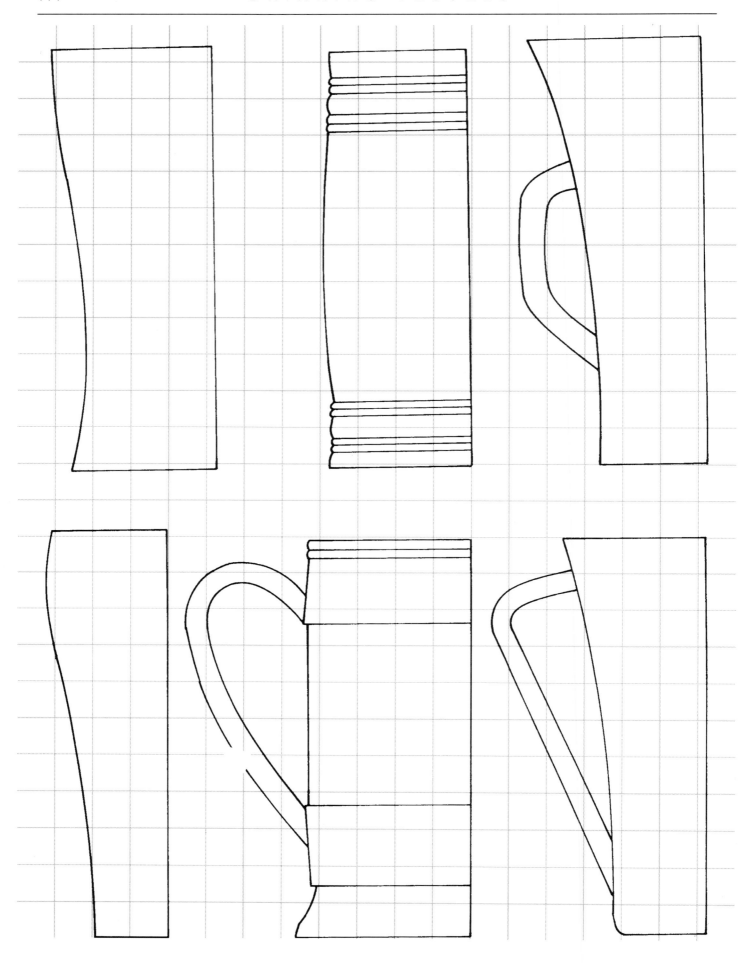

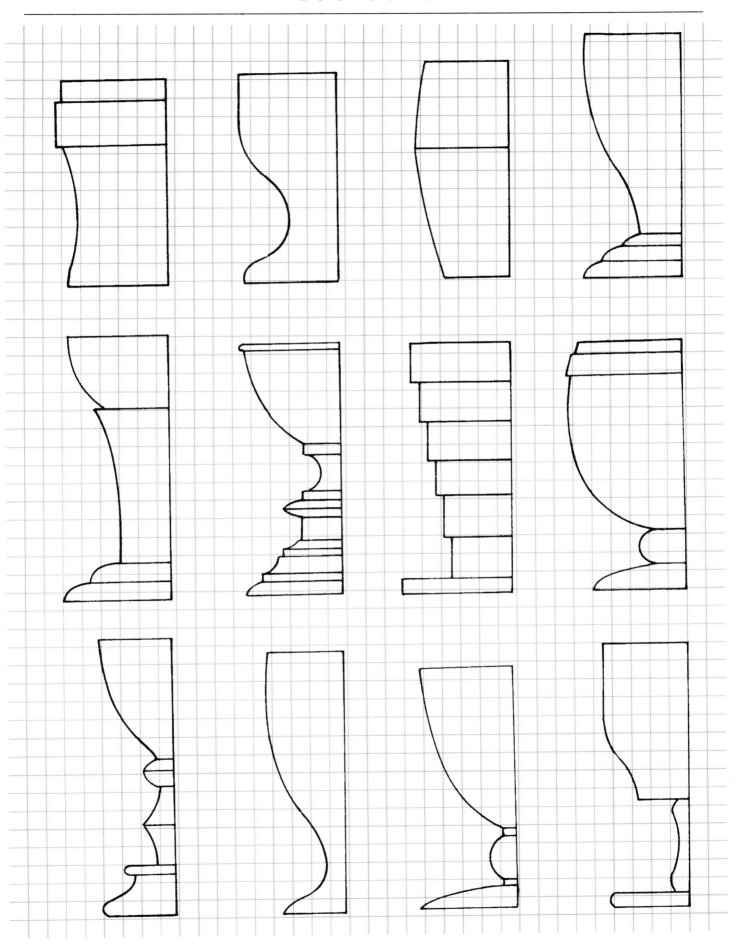

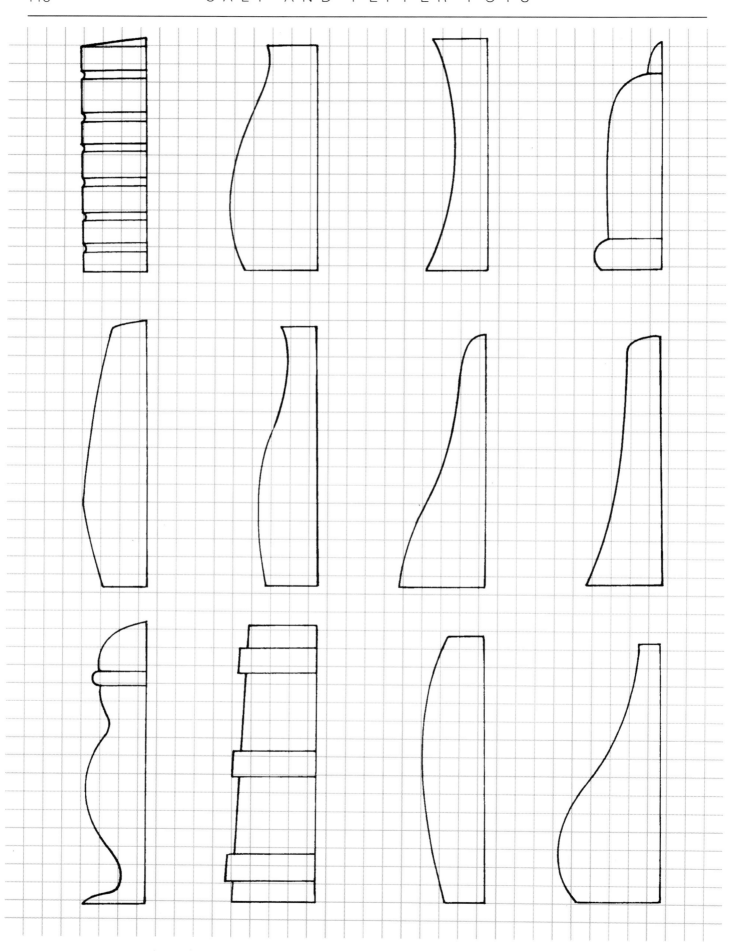

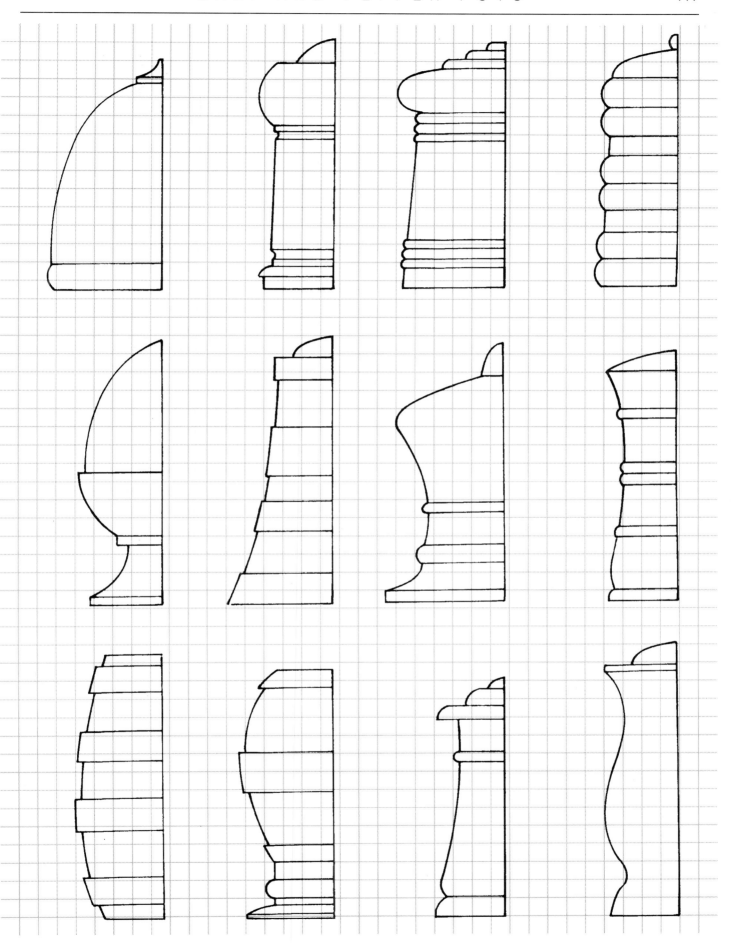

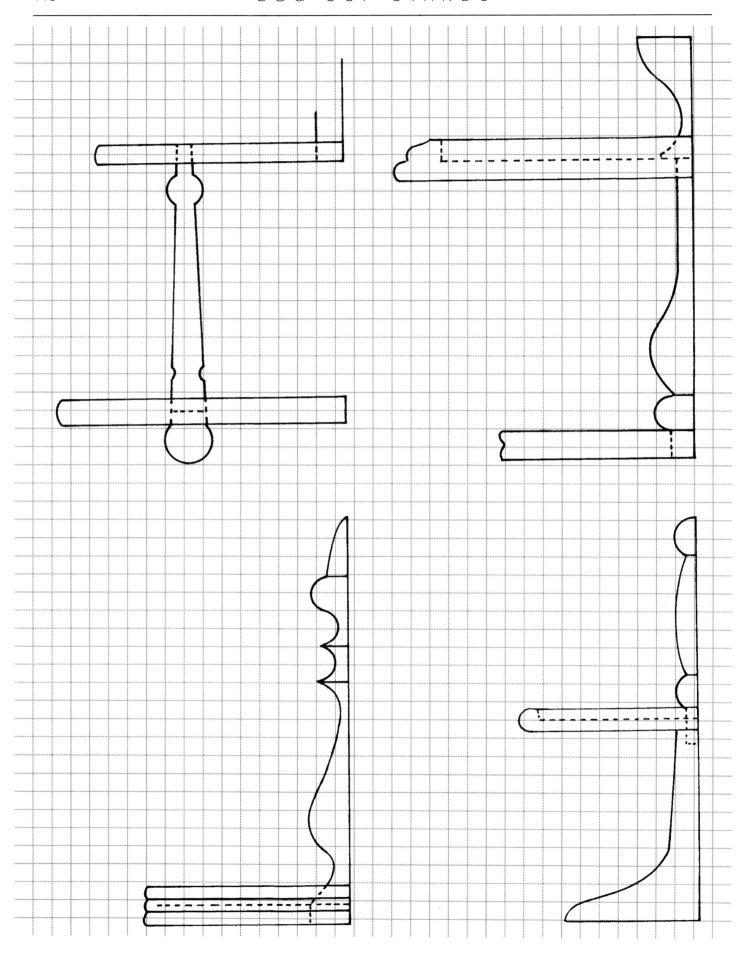

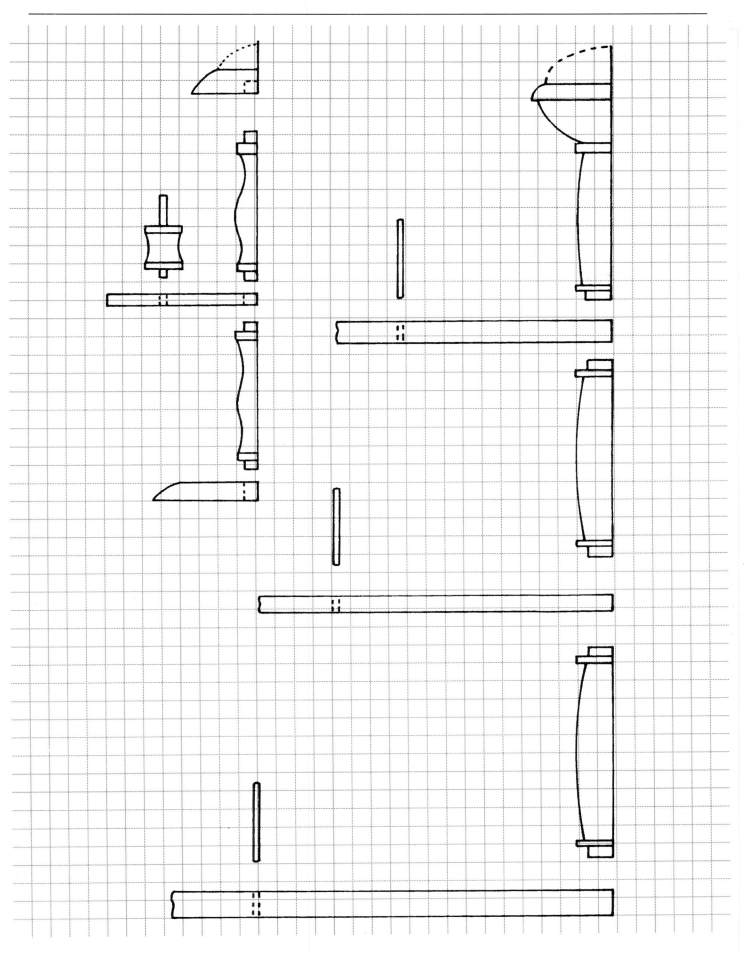

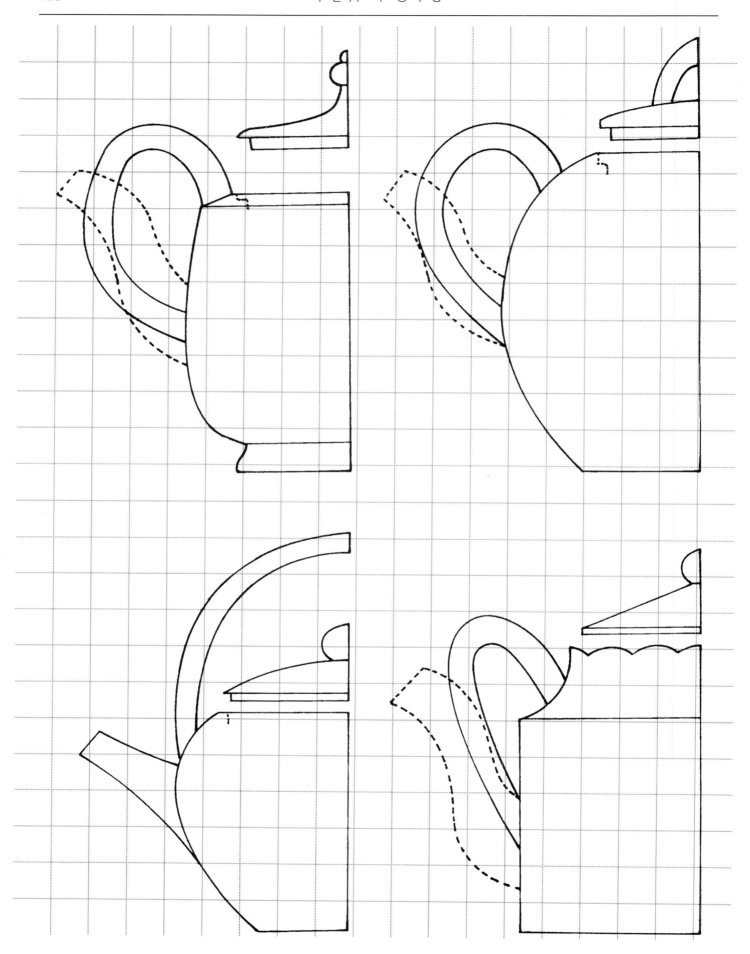

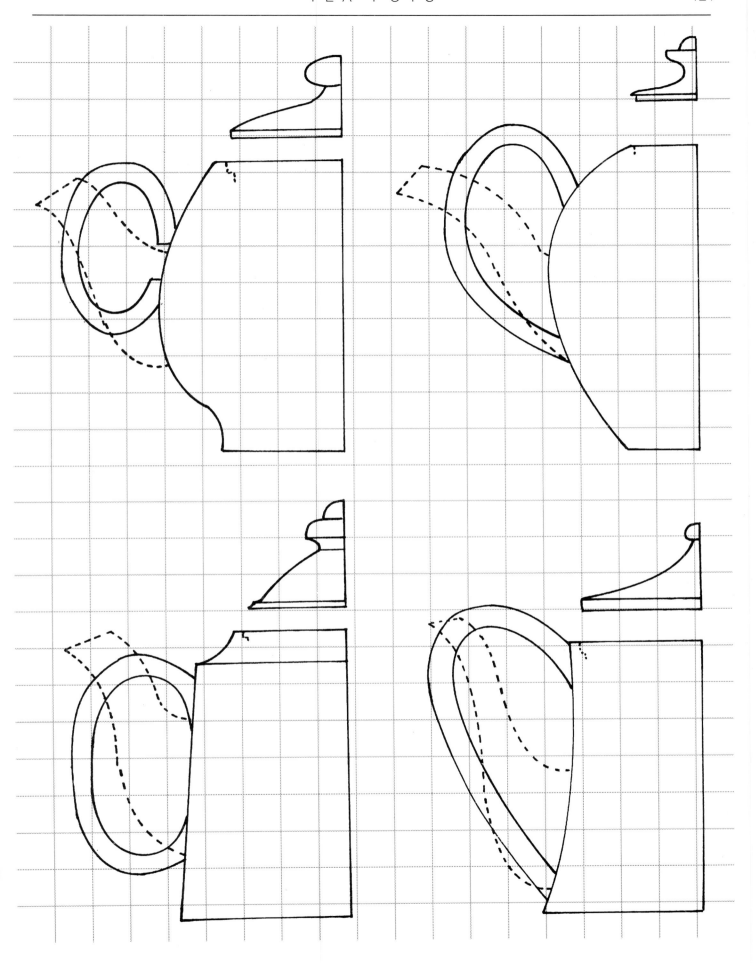

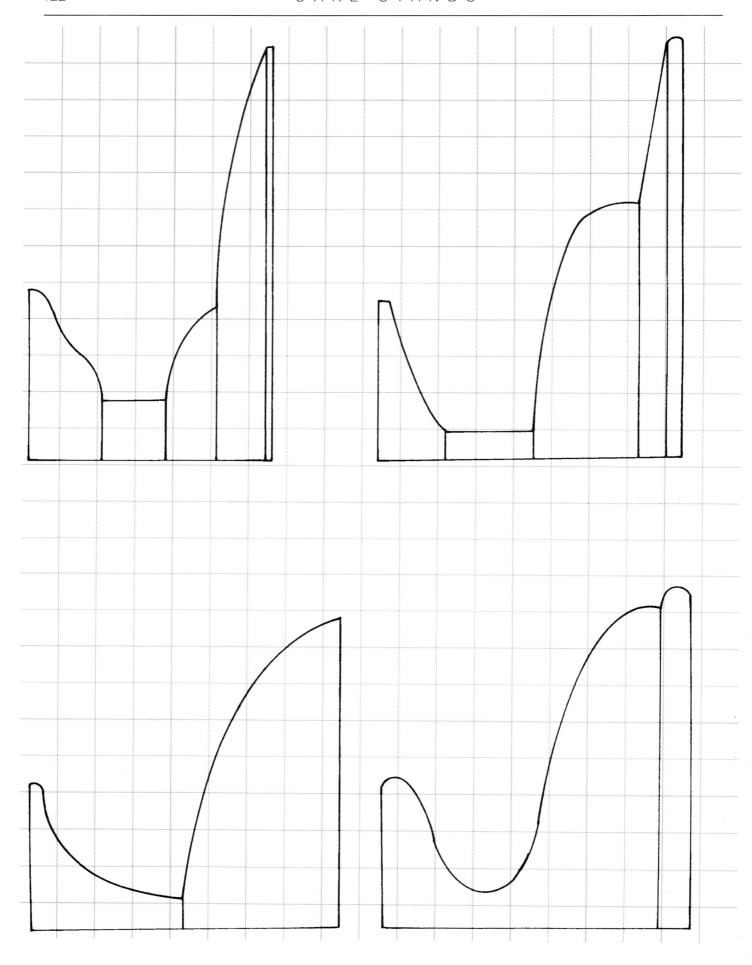

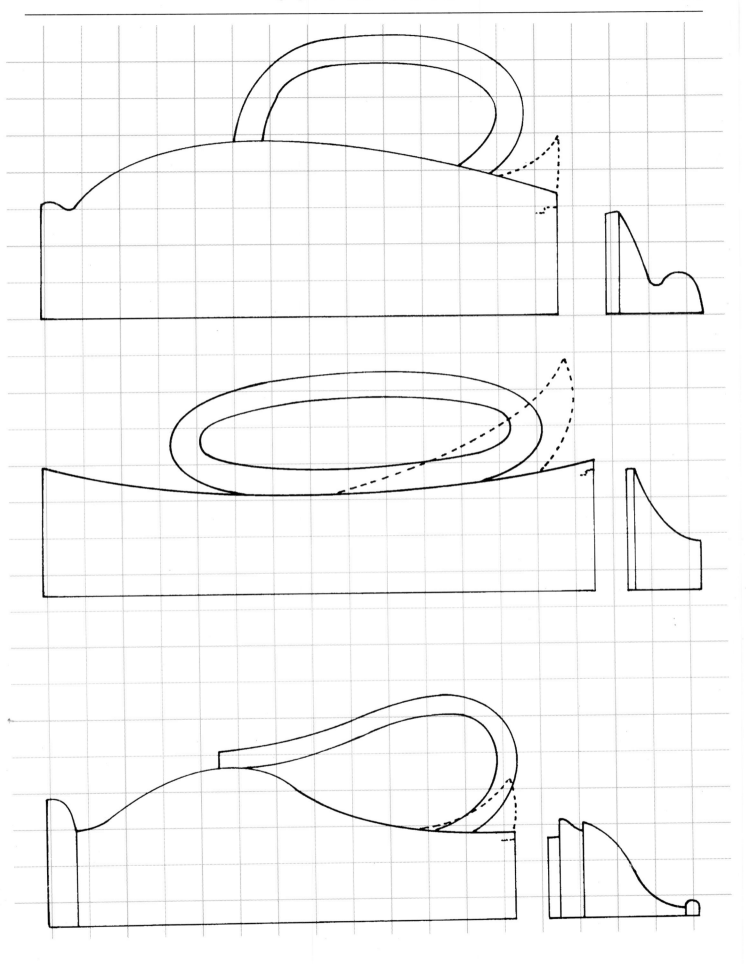

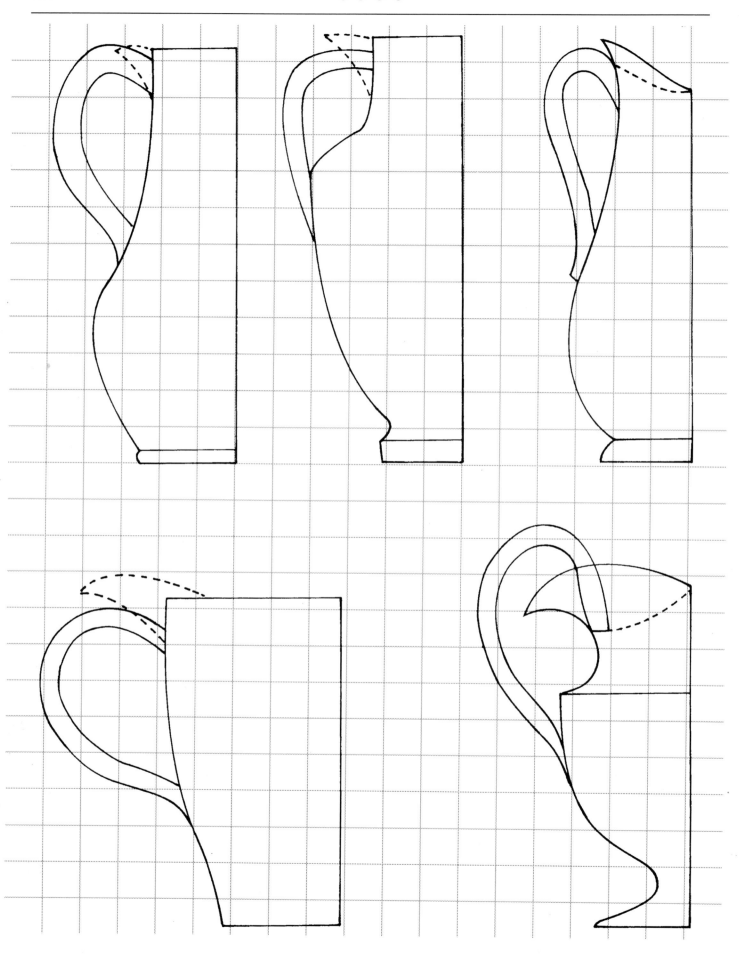

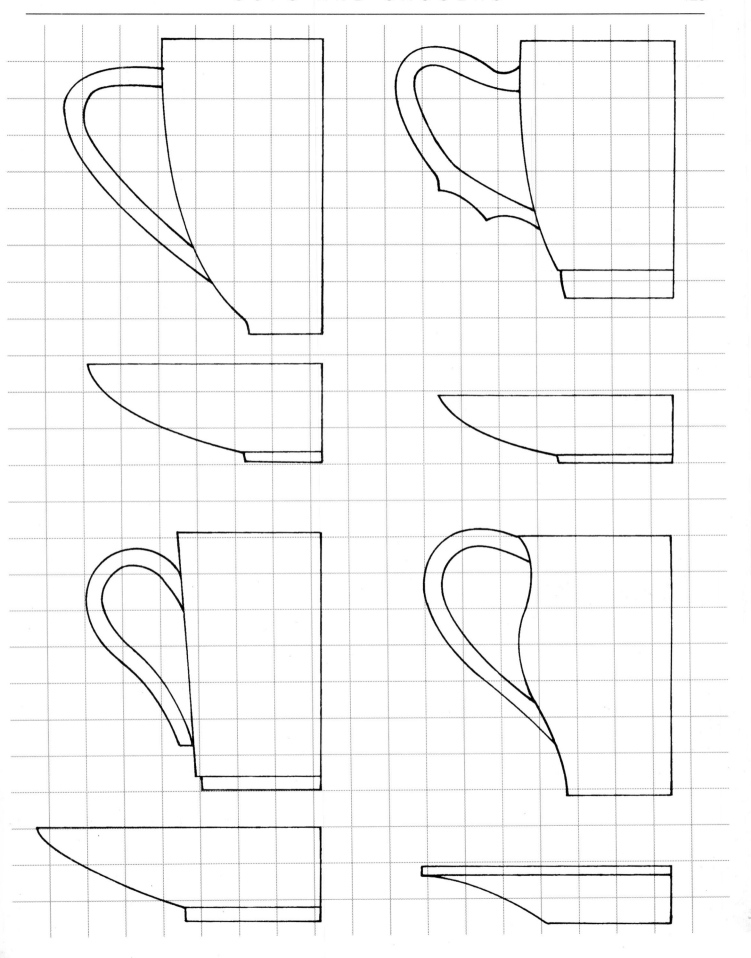

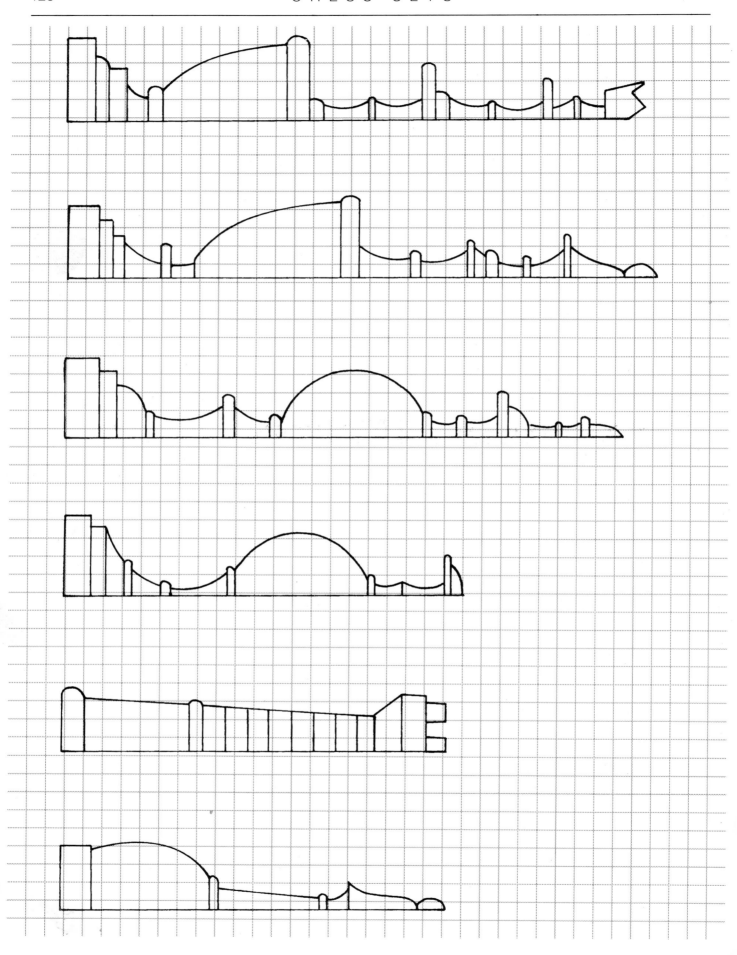

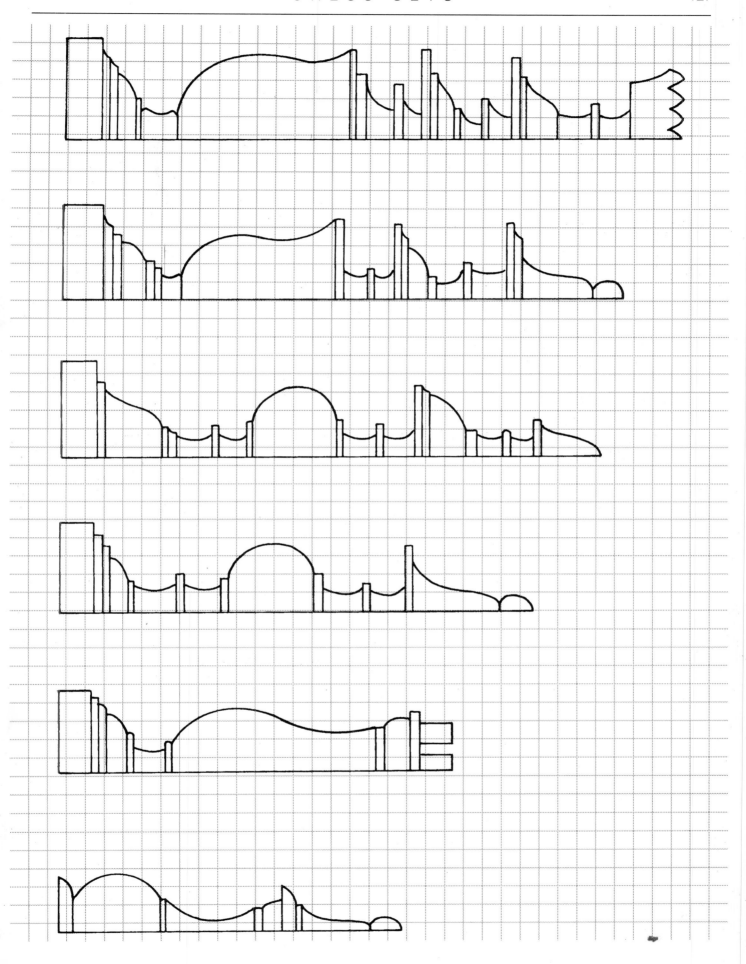

BIBLIOGRAPHY

Child, Peter   *The Craftsman Woodturner*   Bell & Hyman, 1984
Nish,   Dale   *Artistic   Woodturning*   Brigham   Young
University Press, 1975
Nish, Dale   *Creative Woodturning*   Brigham Young University
Press, 1975
Pain, Frank   *The Practical Woodturner*   Evans, 1958
Pracht, Klaus   *Woodturning*   Dryad, 1988
Sainsbury, John   *The Craft of Woodturning*   Sterling, 1984
Sainsbury, John   *Guide to Woodturning Tools and Equipment*
David & Charles, 1989
Stokes, Gordon   *The Manual of Woodturning*   Pelham, 1979
Wooldridge, W.J.   *Woodturning*   Batsford, 1982